# What

*"Kelly's book is a heartfelt message to all of us that there is nothing that can stop us from moving ahead. Her inspirational story of being a survivor, a mother, a wife and speaker will help anyone reading to feel that they too can do whatever they set their mind to do."*

**Cheryl Cran,** CSP Creator of Your Keynote Coach
www.yourkeynotecoach.com
Leadership & Generations Expert www.cherylcran.com

*"Kelly has refused to be overcome by a life-threatening and life-changing childhood accident. When you think your life has been difficult you need to be thinking in your mind the answer compared to what? Read this book as Kelly shares her most deepest pain and inner experiences with you on every page. Her authenticity will deeply touch, move and inspire you in ways only you will know deep inside yourself once you experience reading this book. I had tears along the way while reading this book. In my personal opinion, this book is a positive Game Changer for your life. Start reading it today."*

**Darren Jacklin,** World Class Professional Speaker,
Corporate Trainer, Best-Selling Author, Television Celebrity
http://www.DarrenJacklin.com

*"I have watched Kelly grow through the years and what an amazing effort she has put into her passion. She is fierce, determined, motivated, energetic and lets nothing get in her way. As they say "birds of a feather flock together." I hope Kelly will let me sit in her nest. Go for GOLD!!*

**Michelle Peavy**
www.michellepeavy.com

*"You are an amazing person, Kel and I am very proud to say that you are my cousin. Love you!"*

**Rod Cheresnuik**

*"Incredible! Absolutely incredible Kelly! I could actually feel my gut wrenching while reading your mom's letter, as I imagined what a hell it would have been for us if it happened to our daughter. I also admire all that you have been through in your life. It would have been easy for you to do nothing. People would understand, instead you are such a go-getter with such an amazing attitude. Thanks for sharing this with all of us!"*

**Allan Marston**

# No Risk

## *No Rewards*

**KELLY FALARDEAU**

**To contact Kelly Falardeau:**
Website: www.mykellyf.com
Blog: http://blog.mykellyf.com

To my kids, Alexanna, Cody and Parker:

You three are the biggest inspiration in my life.
Find your dreams and follow your passion,
because if you don't, nobody else will do it for you.

*"Dreams are meant to be found,
Not tucked away in Dreamland."*

# A Word from the Author

*"If you want more possibilities in life, you have to take the risk in order to gain the rewards."*

*"Even though I wasn't considered one of the "pretty girls" I still tried out for the cheerleading squad, I still tried out for choir, I still asked the guys to dance, and I still put myself out there because I knew that I wouldn't get anywhere in life if I just stayed home and continued to be shy and blamed everything on my scars. Eventually people started saying that they didn't notice my scars, they noticed my inner beauty."*

*"Ultimately, life is about choices. You can choose to be happy or you can choose to be sad. You can choose to feel ugly or you can choose to feel beautiful. You can choose to believe that people are staring at you because they think you're ugly, or you can choose to think that people think you're beautiful or just curious about what happened. You can choose to follow your dreams, or you can choose to feel sorry for yourself because others get their dreams and you don't. You can choose to walk out that door no matter what others think, or you can choose to hide inside because you think you don't deserve a life. I choose life!"*

# Table of Contents

# Foreword

To say this book by Kelly Falardeau is inspiring would be a huge understatement! It touches parts of your heart you probably don't know even exists. It can make you cry and then have your heart soaring high and wanting to be like her as she shares her victories. She has proven beyond any doubt that anyone can overcome life's challenges. It is a fabulous resource for truths that can help anyone struggling with any kind of life struggles!

Though it is fun and easy to read, it addresses and solves a big problem that far too many people have. How you see yourself is crucial to happiness and success. If you think your choices are limited and that you feel like a victim of circumstances and of life then you need to read this book. Kelly proves that everyone has choices and even if your background has been tough or lacking in some way, you can choose to make changes and create success.

If you feel that life has not been fair to you and that you are a victim of less than good circumstances, bad parenting, or ignorance and are constantly facing problem after problem with no end in sight, this book is perfect for you. It will show you how to change everything around... and quickly.

If you want to go to the next level of success but feel stymied or stuck, this book can help you get unstuck and start moving towards that success you long for and deserve.

As an internationally recognized success expert I can say, without reservation that Kelly has done a great job in explaining how what life throws at you doesn't have to keep you down! Read it NOW!

*Jack M. Zufelt*
*"Mentor to Millions"*
*Author of the #1 best selling book,*
**The DNA of Success**, *International Keynote Speaker and*
*Trainer* www.dnaofsuccess.com
www.jackzufeltspeaks.com

# Introduction

I have divided this book into two parts, the first part is all about me, how I got burnt and some pivotal events in my life, and the second part is all about what makes me tick, motivates me to be who I am and how I have become the *successful* me.

I started writing this book with Part Two first because I wanted to make it a business-oriented book. I was focusing on 10-key topics that helped me become successful, but then I realized that people would want to know how I got burnt and how I became the strong me that I am today. I realized that I would have to add in the stories of how I got burnt, went from being the ugly scar-faced girl to the beautiful **Fierce Woman of the Year** (2010), and how I became so confident.

Throughout my book you will find letters from my mother that tell my story better than I ever could. Ultimately, I feel like my Mom is the true hero in my story. I couldn't imagine having to go through the traumatic events and pain she had to live with every day, my scars were a constant reminder to her. The pain she felt when the tragic accident happened, until now, has never left her. My Mom was only 21 when I got burnt. She had already given up a baby for adoption when she was 16, had me at 19, almost lost me at 21 and was also pregnant with my sister at the time, which she was worried about losing too. I would like to say, *"Thank you Mom for opening up your heart and sharing your story, I know it was difficult for you to do this, I hope you will finally be able to release the guilt you feel. I love you and you are an awesome Mom."*

I want to thank my friend Ted Moorhouse and fellow burn survivor friend Jamie Evans for spending countless hours proofreading and helping me to make my book sound great. They both did a tremendous job helping me and without them I wouldn't have been able to make this book come to life.

Ted and I worked together many years ago and lost touch for over 20-years, but then found each other on the internet. What I truly enjoyed about finding Ted was that he recounted how we worked together, and how he never saw my scars, that they were never an issue, and that he always thought I was a beautiful woman. When I told Ted I was writing a book he graciously offered to help me with it. *"Thanks Ted – I am forever grateful and honoured that you took time away from your business and family to help me."*

Jamie Evans and I also go back many years. She is a burn survivor who I met at burn camp 12-years ago. When I met Jamie she was a camper and I had just had my daughter two months earlier. I brought my daughter to burn camp with me because I wanted to inspire the other campers to have their own families if that was what they wanted. If I could have a baby, they could too. Jamie told me years later, that I did indeed inspire her to have kids of her own and now she has three kids too, a girl and two boys just like I have. *"Thanks Jamie – I am also forever grateful that you wanted to help me with my book as I know you had other deadlines of your own, plus your family to take care of."*

Most importantly, I want to thank my family. Especially my husband Max, my daughter Alexanna, my sons Cody and Parker, my sister Kim and her husband Tim, niece Abbey, my Mom Jean and my step-dad Don; without them, my life would not be the way it is today. And of course I would like to recognize my cousin Rod – Rod knows I never ever blamed him for getting burnt and I know the tragedy is just as fresh in his mind as my Mom's. *"Mom and Rod, quit worrying so much, I became a success even with the scars."*

I also want to give a special thank you to Stephen Williams and Nadine Spindler of the Canadian Burn Foundation, they have sponsored many of the trips I have taken to burn camps and burn conferences around the world. To help this great organization, visit their website at www.CanadianBurnFoundation.org.

I want to thank my husband Max because he took the risk to love me when others wouldn't. He stood beside me when I came up with my crazy ideas and he encouraged me to move forward and be me. He encouraged me to feel beautiful about myself and whenever I needed help, he was there to get me through it. *"Thanks Max, couldn't have done it without you, love you too!"*

One of the reasons I want to acknowledge my step-dad Don, is because as much as we had a challenging relationship throughout the years, ultimately, it was that relationship that made me fight for my life and gave me my drive to succeed. When he said I couldn't do something, it drove me to want to do it even more; I couldn't quit, and let him win. I had to fight and prove him wrong. *"Thank you Don for giving me that, it made me the strong woman I am and I'm sorry for all the trouble I caused you."*

I also want to thank some of my friends Lee Horbachewski, Charmaine Hammond, Michelle Peavy, Cindy Rutter, Rachel Gour, Jo Ann Vacing, Dianna Bowes, Michele Weselake, Rhonda Schumm, Sherri Scott, Sherri Tirschmann, Cheryl Cran, Sharon Pandza, Trisha Ladouceur, Marlie Anderson, Debra Kasowski, Janeen Norman, Tamara Plant, Dawn Ofner, Devon Augade, Stephen Williams, Nadine Spindler, Lynda Fraser and the countless others for helping me and encouraging me to tell my story and come out into the spotlight. I know I've forgotten a few, there's so many more to recognize, please forgive me. I honestly didn't feel I had a story to tell until a year ago, but now I realize what my story is about.

When I spoke at the World Burn Congress last October, I listened to the keynote speakers and was totally humbled that the Phoenix Society (http://www.phoenix-society.org/) felt my story was worthy enough to be at their conference. They asked me to speak on two different topics.

After I listened to the first keynote speaker, I had to leave the room so I could have a meltdown and I sent a text to my best friend telling him about the keynote and how honoured and humbled I was, but didn't feel like I had anything to offer the burn survivors that were at the conference. My friend reminded me that I had a purpose, I had to speak, and I had a story that people want to hear. I was crying and couldn't see where I was going, but I kept walking and walking until I stopped at the end of the street and looked up at the street sign – the sign said "Hope Boulevard" and I was reminded at that point what my purpose really was. **My purpose was to give people hope; hope that they too can have a normal and fulfilling life even as a burn survivor.** I went back and took a picture of that street sign so I could blog about it. **I believe my story is about Hope.**

This book is about the journey of my many risks and adventures in life; starting with walking out the door and facing the staring and teasing in order to gain a life. Everyone deserves a life no matter what you look like. This book is also about me once *feeling* like the ugly duckling and *turning* into the beautiful swan over the many years of living and struggling to overcome the odds. I hope you enjoy reading it as much as I enjoyed writing it. In the words of Jimmy Johnson, *"If you quit now, you'll miss out on the big reward later."*

My book doesn't always run in sequence, and you may hear one story more than once or maybe it will be started at one point in the book and ended in another point. This book was written by me and then I had some awesome friends of mine proof read it and correct the errors. I intended on having a professional editor work with my book, but I wanted my story to be in my own words. **I hope you enjoy reading about my life, as told by me.**

# PART ONE – My Life as ME

I am a woman, mother, wife, aunt, sister, step-sister, half-sister, sister-in-law, author, entrepreneur, speaker and burn survivor. **I am me, and the best me that I can be.** I was burnt when I was two years old, which was the first indication that I was a survivor. When I got burnt, my parents and family thought I was going to die, with the exception of my Popa [my grandpa, my Mom's dad]. He always said that there was some reason I lived.

There was no way a two year old with 75% burns could live without a purpose in this life. Somehow I made it, and so I'm also a survivor; a survivor who doesn't quit and thrives on doing the impossible. I am Kelly, the burn survivor.

I admire people who have one job forever and know who they want to be, but I am definitely not one of those people. I have NEVER known who or what I wanted to be. I never had a career picked out; and I still don't. I have done a million things, and know I will do a million more in my lifetime. I'm not totally sure what they will be, but I do know that I have a lot more living to do. I'm excited about what other opportunities will interest and challenge me in the future.

As a teenager, there were many nights when I would go to bed hoping that I would not wake up in the morning, or if I had to wake up, could I at least wake up without scars on my face? Could I at least wake up and not be ugly? Could I at least have a normal life like all the pretty girls, not having to worry about being teased, stared at or whispered about?

All of my life I struggled with the whole "beauty concept," and what being beautiful meant. I was told that my scars would never go away and that the only way to fix me would be to wear make-up to cover the scars. There was no magic surgery my doctor could perform to make my scars go away for good.

I hated make-up, without really knowing it at the time. I hated the feel of it on my face. When I looked in the mirror, I saw my Mom's pain. She knew I just wanted to be beautiful, and the only way she knew how to help me was by putting make-up on me. I only wanted to wear it on special occasions, as maybe just once, people would notice me without my scars and say I was beautiful. I was tired of hearing how beautiful I was from my Mom, Nana or aunt. I was beautiful to them, no matter what I looked like. I just wanted to hear that I was beautiful from someone other than my family.

I wanted some guy in school to say, *"Wow, you're beautiful,"* but that never happened (at least not in high school). I didn't know it at the time, but the guys were too afraid to step out of their comfort zones. They were afraid of what their friends would think of them if they liked the "ugly scar-faced" girl.

I'll never forget one of the dates I did go on in high school. It wasn't a real date, but it was the closest thing to a real date I had experienced, because it was just him and I and not my usual group. He was my friend's brother, and he was going to a party. My friend asked me if I'd go with her brother, and I said sure, originally she was supposed to go too, but she got a better option. It was a night I'll never forget. I was in grade-12; I picked out my best jeans then I had my Mom do my make-up so that none of my scars were showing. Even though I hated the feel of the make-up, my Mom did a great job making me look beautiful. I secretly hoped somebody would notice. I still remember my Mom's last words that evening, *"Kel, this is the best I can do covering up your scars."*

He picked me up and we went to the party. There were only 10 people there, including us. Six of them were in the kitchen doing drugs and the four of us remaining were in the living room trying to decide whether we were staying there or going to another party. Eventually, the other couple decided to go home, and so my date took me home too. I was thoroughly disappointed that there weren't more people there to show the new *'beautiful me'* to.

When I got home, I told my Mom that I wasn't comfortable being there since everyone, but us four, were doing drugs. The truth was, I felt like a complete dork getting all made-up for absolutely nothing. My Mom was so happy that I had the guts to leave a party that had drugs at it, but little did she know all the parties I went to had drugs at them, I just chose not to do them.

The next day, my friend said that her brother told her I didn't look like I had a good time and was disappointed. I was, but I didn't let her know that. I just told her that there weren't a lot of people there. I would have been happier going out with my usual group of friends.

**A lesson learned**: there is no sense getting all made up for nothing. This was the first, and last time I went through the trouble of covering up all my scars just to make other people happy and see that I was beautiful. I would just have to learn how to feel beautiful without make-up and without feeling like I was wearing a mask.

# MASK OR NO MASK

Mask because others would think I'm beautiful, or no mask and risk what others think of me? A mask; yes, that's what I felt like. I felt like I was wearing a mask, trying to be someone I wasn't. I didn't need a mask to hide my scars or the real me. I didn't need to be hidden; I needed to find a way to feel beautiful without make-up.

My Nana told me a long time ago about how one day she was talking to a friend of hers. We had just gotten home from shopping and her friend said, *"You take her out in public?"* My Nana replied to her friend, *"Yes, of course we take her out in public. We are not ashamed of her, she is our grand-daughter and we love her no matter what she looks like."*

I often wonder about other burn survivors who wear that heavy make-up that makes their faces look so white and truly like they're wearing a mask; why do they wear it? I know they want to cover their scars because they think it makes them look more beautiful. But, seriously, does it really?

Whenever I see them, I always wonder what they would look like without it. Maybe they would look better without it. But, I suppose what I really want to know is why people are so determined to wear make-up just so someone else can think they are beautiful? How many more people actually tell you they think you look more beautiful when you're wearing it? I seriously do not understand why make-up makes some women feel better, when it makes me feel so terrible. Maybe I don't understand because I was burnt when I was two, and I don't know myself any other way, so I don't understand the need to look any different than I do.

I don't like the idea of wearing a mask because then I would have to spend 30- to 60-minutes every morning putting it on. And let's face it; I'm not a morning person and if it takes me more than 15-minutes to get ready, then I'm not doing it.

I certainly don't see a need to spend an hour doing make-up just so someone else can think I'm beautiful. I would rather people get used to seeing me the way I am without make-up. I told myself many times that people would just have to learn to accept my looks the way they are; simple as that. No mask for me.

The bottom line is that people have to do whatever makes them feel happy and beautiful. If wearing make-up makes you feel great; then absolutely wear it. If it doesn't make you feel great, then don't wear it. I know that wearing more than mascara and lip gloss doesn't make me feel great at all, so I don't wear it.

# THE TRAGIC ACCIDENT

Obviously, you're wondering what happened, how did Kelly get burnt? I thought the best way to tell the story of the tragic accident would be with a letter from my Mom.

*November 23, 2010*

*Dear Kel,*

*This is the hardest letter that I have ever had to write. You should realize that this was the biggest life-changing day of my life, August 28, 1968.*

*There was nothing that I could do to change that horrible day, no matter what. It was only 15-minutes in time that, no matter what, could never be changed. How horrible, I couldn't apologize, plead, beg, and bribe my way out of this terrifying accident. It was the most painful, hurtful, go to hell and back day.*

*I just had your cousins Michael, Rod & you in for supper and you all wanted to go back outside and the boys wanted to keep throwing the old shingles off of the garage roof into the burning barrel. If only I had kept you back to change your diaper, if only, if only, if only, I could say it a million times but it would still not change anything that happened to you.*

*I heard the boys making noise, you crying and our neighbor Willie had just driven into the yard. I ran outside to see what was going on; you were on the steps at Nana's house. Your shirt was still on fire and so I put my hand on it & put it out. Willie had poured the water on you that Rod had got to put out the fire. The boys said you were on the far side of the burning barrel and came around the barrel & you were on fire. They didn't want to roll you in the dirt that would make you dirty, so Rod went to get water.*

*You were crying & crying, it was horrible, I picked you up and ran with you to our house, I wrapped a blanket around you & away we went, Willie, you & I to the Stony Plain Hospital.*

*We arrived at emergency and called Dr Ringham to come to the hospital. Dr Ringham saw you & did as much as he could to make you comfortable and told us to take you as fast as we could to the University of Alberta Hospital. The doctor would call ahead and let them know we were coming. They called the police for an escort, but we never found them.*

*We drove so fast that it only took us 20-minutes from Stony Plain Hospital to the U of A Hospital and normally it takes 45. On the way, you said to me, "Mommy it hurts." That just ripped my heart out & threw it on the floor, I was crying all the while. I replied, "Yes I know baby. We are getting you help as soon as possible." The three of us were terrified.*

*The three doctors and multiple nurses were all waiting for us, when we arrived at the hospital. The doctor scooped you out of my arms and I never saw you again until the next day. Someone took me and put me into an office in the emergency area of the hospital and forgot about me. All I could do was pray, pray and pray, I was so frightened. I knew nothing for hours. This was around 7:30 pm when we hit the hospital.*

*Your Dad came to the hospital & could not find me. Nana & Popa came to the hospital, they couldn't find me either. I was 21, barefoot and pregnant. No shoes on and no identification. I don't know what happened to Willie, he couldn't find me either.*

*Finally after about three hours, Dr. Henry Shimizu came into the room where I was & told me what was going on, and where you were & how seriously you were burned. I don't really have a clue as to what he said other than he told me you had a 50/50 chance of living. All I could imagine was someone flipping a coin saying heads you live, tails you lose.*

*They took you up to surgery to put a tracheotomy in your throat so you could breathe. Seventy-five percent of your body was burned and 35% was into the flesh, beyond third degree. Then he left me and I didn't see him again for days. I was flabbergasted.*

*I was in shock. I just could not understand why this would happen, what had I done to deserve such punishment? Was it because I was such a rebellious teenager, but if that was the case why punish my child? Why not me? I wanted to change places with you & would have, if I could have. This was just insane. All alone, no one anywhere, what was I to do? My brain was going a 100 mph. Where were my parents, my husband, someone to rescue me, wake me up & tell me this is all a bad dream? This can't be true. Terrible things don't happen to people like us. I could not make heads nor tails of what, in heavens name, was going on. This is so unbelievable.*

*Please God, what can I do to change this horrible tragedy? What, how, when, why, how do I change this? I don't know what to do. What about my beautiful baby Kelly Ann, my beautiful baby. Please God, don't take her from me I just got her two years ago, don't take this baby away from me too. Kelly is so wonderful, happy, smiley, so pure, so good, so innocent. Why my child? The only good thing in my life & you want to take her away from me, I don't understand. Why is life so cruel? What's going on? This is terrifying, please stop the world & let me off. Let me go back to yesterday, I will do anything to change this day. What can I do??? Panic is not the word, for what I was feeling.*

*Finally your Dad found me; it was around midnight or so. He wanted to know what happened, he wanted to kill the boys. Well, it took a lot of talking to stop that from happening. The nurses would not let us see you because you were in the operating room and they didn't know when you would be in a room. They took our phone number & said they would call if anything happened. We left the hospital in shock.*

*Your Dad drove home. We were both bargaining with God to change things, but no dice. It is so sick. This can't be happening. On the way home the song "You are my Precious Angel" came on the radio, I was crying my eyes out. To this day, I still cry when I hear that song. I can now play it on the piano, but it takes a lot to stop the tears.*

*Well, we got home and Nana and Popa [my Mom's parents] were still up waiting for us. Since the day you were born, Nana had a premonition that something horrible was going to happen to you. She was always worried about you. The boys had come into the house & gone to bed, they were terrified also. As far as all of us were concerned, this was the world's worst day.*

*Popa phoned Aunty Audrey and Uncle Robert, [my Mom's sister and brother] and they all came home the next day to be with us. Your Dad phoned Uncle Bob, [my dad's brother] who was living in Vancouver with Aunty Janice. Your other Nana, Nana T [my Dad's mom] was there with him on vacation. Nana T had been to a tea-cup reader the day before and the reader told Nana T that a tragedy was going to happen soon. She was sick; she didn't think anything was really going to happen.*

*We were a very close family in those days. We prayed together. The neighbours knew what was going on and so they sent food, best wishes, and came visiting. We called the hospital the next day; you had made it through the night. You were in the Pediatrics-Intensive care unit # 36 of the old hospital. Nurse Rohatten was the charge nurse. You had nurses' care 24-hours a day. You were very serious. You were nowhere out of danger.*

*Aunty Audrey & Uncle Bill [my mom's sister and brother-in-law] drove up to see you the next day. Uncle Robert was on his way too. Your nurse would not let me into your room because your face was so swollen like a football. It had retained the fluids to cool off the burns on your face. The nurse also didn't want you getting too excited by seeing us. These things I found out later. We were only there for a short time, you were also in shock and trying very hard to stay alive. Reluctantly, we left the hospital.*

*Dr. Ringham called to see how I was doing because I was pregnant with Kim at the time, in my seventh month and he wanted to see me. When I went to see him I had lost 16-pounds since my last appointment. The doctor was very concerned about me. He didn't want me to lose this baby too.*

*You made it through the weekend. Finally, they let us see you and you were very excited to see us. You were not abandoned, you still had parents and people that loved you more than you would ever know.*

*We had to gown-up & put on masks. You had three intravenous cut downs into your body, one in your neck area, one in the groin area and one in your ankle. You also had the tracheotomy in your throat but that didn't stop you from talking. You didn't know you were not supposed to be able to talk so you did anyways. The nurses were very glad that you had such a good vocabulary so that they could communicate with you. You were only 25-months old. You were only about 31"-32" tall and when you came in only 26-pounds. You were very tiny. You lost a lot of weight and it was hard for them to keep your weight up. I think you lost about 10-pounds.*

*You had a night nurse that came to stay with you the first night that you were in the hospital and that lady, I never found out who she was, was a little older and you called her Nana. She stayed with you for weeks, even after she was not on the payroll. She came & spent her nights with you because she didn't want to leave you alone. What a wonderful lady and nurse. I would truly like to thank her from the bottom of my heart for her dedication.*

*There were so many ups and downs with you. Every Monday and Friday, Dr. Shimizu would take you into the operating room so that he could de-bride your burns and redress them with donor skin from amputated arms & legs from other people. They took all the skin off of your Dad's leg to cover up the burns on your tiny body. Skin is the best coverage in such a situation no matter where it is from. This was to prevent infection and make the burns a little more bearable for you.*

*As time went by, you got better and didn't need to have 24-hour care so they moved you up to the burn ward on the fourth floor. There you & another little boy who had been burned by 60,000 volts from a power line at Blackfalds shared the same nurse. He had climbed the power poles to get his kite. The voltage killed him, but the sudden stop when he hit the ground started his heart again or otherwise he would have been dead. After a short time you were returned to station 36 again.*

*We did not let Nana and Popa come and visit you in the hospital because they could not have handled seeing you with all your burns. Your burns were unbelievable, and your skin was black and there were temporary grafts everywhere. You had huge pressure bandages on your arms, legs, chest etc. The back of your head was burned and you had a 6" foam donut for a pillow under your head.*

*There was no way Nana and Popa were up to seeing you in such a horrible state, but there was one person that would not stay away and that was your Auntie Bert. Bertha Schumm, she was Nana's best friend. She was visiting her husband in the hospital at the time. He had a stroke and was doing his rehabilitation in the same hospital. She would come up to your room and look in on you and report back to Nana about you. They wouldn't let her in to see you because she was not family, but she would wave to you and you knew your Auntie Bertie. She was always very special to you and I'm sure that is why, what a wonderful lady.*

*Your Dad & I had quite a routine. He would go to work in the morning and I would go to the hospital to visit you around 10 am depending on what day it was & what was happening with you. Your Dad would come after work and he would stay with you until bed time. He would read you a story and put you to bed and all that stuff. We had a TV for you so we all could watch. Some days were long & boring, as the conversations with a two year old are not that long.*

*One day I was down at the snack bar getting something for lunch. I ran into a fellow my brother went to school with. He was working in the hospital and he asked me about you and then made the comment "Boy is she ever going to be scarred." Well what a shocker that was. I wasn't ready for that statement. I just had not thought that far ahead. This was probably in October some time. I have never to this day ever talked to that person again. I couldn't handle it.*

*I don't remember how long it was before we got you out of the hospital, but Dec 15th seems to ring a bell, we brought you home, Auntie Bertie, Uncle Ed, Nana & Popa were all there. Nana had Kim in the car bed in the living room. We came in to the kitchen and everyone was excited to see you, hugs all around. Then you decided to go into the living room. There was a car bed on the floor and you went over to see what was in it. You looked in and then turned around and said, "Mommy, there's a baby in there." I said, "Yes, that is your new baby sister." You were so excited. We were finally all together. It had been a very long haul. You became her biggest advocate, you wanted to hold her, feed her, change her diaper, I couldn't do anything for Kim without you. We shared it all.*

*By this time you had skin grafts on your knees, your face, your chest front & back and the skin on your legs had been donor sites about four times by now. Each time you had to heal so that grafts could be taken again.*

*Dr. Shimizu was a very compassionate doctor. He had all the time in the world for you, but was a little impatient with me & all my questions. I would chase him down the hall asking him questions. You had a long contraction down your right arm from your armpit to your elbow. This was due to that fact that you didn't have enough donor sites. Dr. Shimizu was saving your tummy skin for your face to be used at a later date. We were all well known around the hospital. You were such a beautiful child with gorgeous eyes and an instant smile.*

*When you came home we had to do physiotherapy with your arms and legs so that they wouldn't contract. Every night you and your Dad were in the tub and he was your therapist.*

*My favorite aunt really surprised me. Auntie Patty came from Calgary to visit. She was at the farm many times, but one time she said such a stupid thing. I didn't realize how sheltered people were back in their day. Aunt Patty said to Nana, "You aren't going to take her – meaning you – Kelly out in public are you?" She was afraid for you, not ashamed of you. She loved you with all her heart. I was shocked when Nana told me this, but she just loved you so much and didn't want people to stare and poke fun at you.*

*I would talk with your teachers and they said that you were handling your scars very well with the other children. They were surprised at how much you knew about what happened to you and what made you just a little different. Most kids just accepted what you said and away you went, friends still. Remember, it doesn't matter who you are, young kids will find something different about you just so they can tease someone. There was and always will be bullies, they are very insecure people who think that a good defense is a good offence.*

*You know, I never remember really talking about your burns with all the family. We just all accepted what had happened and continued from there. There was nothing that would change any of it, so go forward make lemonade from the lemons. I never blamed Michael or Rod for your tragedy; I blamed myself, for being so lazy and for not keeping you in the house and changing your diaper. Maybe that would have changed our lives, and if "IFS & BUTS WERE CHRISTMAS NUTS, WE'D ALL HAVE A MERRY CHRISTMAS."*

*I just live with the guilt & the shame of being so stupid. I also blamed your father for not being home that night because you would have been with him. I was too young, too stupid to know the consequences of what the hell you kids were doing.*

*Sorry Kel that is as far as I can go, if there is anything that you want to know, ask me & I will tell you.*

*Lots of love. MoM*

*PS - I cannot read over it, it is too hard. All I want to do is cry, these scabs never heal, I have learned to keep them at an arms length and I hope you understand.*

One question I get asked a lot is if I remember the accident. I do not remember anything until after I was five years old, in fact, I didn't even remember the accident. When I was five, I started to remember my surgeries, but somehow forgot how I got burnt.

My plastic surgeon Dr. Shimizu needed me to grow more so that my natural skin would stretch so that he would have more skin to use for the rest of my scars and this is why he waited so long between surgeries. Every second year, I spent a month of my summer holidays in the hospital right up until grade-12.

This was not a very fun way to spend the summer, especially when my birthday was also in July. My Mom spent every day in the hospital with me. She never missed a day, no matter how miserable I got, she was there by my side. She also learned how to change my dressings in order to be my personal nurse when I was discharged. My Mom was a tremendous woman who never left my side.

You're probably wondering what happened to my Dad, wasn't he in the hospital with Mom too? Well, my parents divorced when I was five years old and he moved across Canada for a job promotion a few years later. He couldn't always be there for my surgeries, but he always sent me flowers.

I remember one time, going in for surgery and Dr. Shimizu was supposed to do a "Z" plasty under both of my arms and my right wrist and possibly something on two of my fingers to release the contractions. When it was time for the bandages to come off, we never knew what kind of surprise we were in for. A lot of times even Dr. Shimizu forgot what he did on me in the operating room. This  time, when the bandages came off, we noticed he did under my arms and my wrist but not my fingers.

The next surgery, he was supposed to do a skin graft under both my arms and my right wrist because I couldn't lift my arms very high, neither could I move my thumb very well. And my two fingers on my right hand were contracted too.

I'll never forget the day Mom and I went back to the hospital to get my bandages taken off. I remember Mom and I saying to each other, *"I wonder what he did this time?"* This time he had done skin grafts under both my arms, my right wrist AND my two fingers. Only this time he forgot that he had done skin grafts on my fingers. He said to us, *"Oh yeah, I forgot, I did your fingers too."* My Mom and I just laughed and then I started bawling my eyes because I saw these huge gaping holes where the grafts were in my wrist and fingers and wondered if they would ever look normal again.

I always hated when I had to get my bandages off because that also meant he had to take my stitches out and that meant pain. If I had a skin graft, there would be two sets of bandages. One set where the graft was (and that meant the stitches had to be removed) and the second set was the donor site bandages (no stitches on donor sites). Those bandages just fell off naturally when they were healed. I could always tell when they were healing, the donor sites would get really itchy and of course I wasn't allowed to scratch because we didn't want to damage the donor sites. A few days after the itching started, the bandages would fall off and the donor sites were completely healed.

For those of you who don't know, very simply explained, a skin graft is when they remove skin from one part of your body and put it somewhere else. So when my doctor wanted to put skin grafts under both of my arms, wrist and fingers, he took two grafts from my upper inner thighs and used the skin to place on the areas he wanted to fix. So that's why you have two sets of bandages, you have two areas that need to heal, the graft sites and the donor sites. This means, that for the last surgery I was talking about, I had my whole upper body wrapped in bandages, plus my right wrist, fingers, and both my upper legs.

There was no such thing as dissolving stitches back in the 70's, therefore after a few weeks of my grafts healing, I would have to go back to the hospital for my stitches to be removed. I couldn't understand why there wasn't something they could give me to ease the pain of him digging in to the scabs and snipping my stitches. A lot of the times I had over 200 stitches for one surgery. I'm sure it was very difficult for my Mom to watch my doctor inflict pain in order to take out my stitches even though I was a tough kid. I don't know why they didn't give me the pain killers before they took out my stitches.

I also remember another surgery, this one I was in high school. My doctor decided it was time to even out my breasts as one was smaller and quite a bit lower than the other one. He decided he would take the skin from both sides of my right leg and put grafts under each of my breasts. The first time in my life I had to wear a bra. He asked my Mom to buy me a bra so that after he did the skin grafts, he could bandage me up and then put the bra on over top so that my grafts would be held in place. I looked goofy for a while, but it must have worked.

I remember my doctor telling my mom and I that he wasn't even sure if I would have breasts because when you're about two these little cones develop internally and they determine how big your breasts will be. Since I got burnt when I was two, he wasn't sure if I developed the cones or not. I must have because although my breasts weren't very big after the initial surgery, they did grow bigger after each pregnancy.

Although he did a great job on the skin grafts of my breasts, my donor sites didn't do well at all. They ended up scarring tremendously and getting very raised. I had to wear pressure garments on this leg for over a year, in order to help reduce the scarring. I wasn't very happy with this because it also meant I couldn't ride my horse for the summer and compete in horse shows. My doctor decided that my skin had had enough and there would be no more skin grafts for me, four times over was more than my body wanted to take.

My very last set of surgeries included reducing some scarring around my neck. Because of the contractions around my neck, the scars were tight and I didn't have as much mobility around my neck, my skin constantly pulled my chin down and felt tight. In order to loosen the skin and get rid of the scarring, my doctor decided to use tissue expanders to expand the skin and then use that skin to move up and cut off the old scarring.

Tissue expanders are basically an empty silicone implant just like they use for breast implants, except they have a valve attached so that they can be filled up with saline to help expand the skin. I was only the second person in my province to try this procedure.

The first time my doctor tried it, it worked well for a couple months, but then because the tissue expander was so tight, my doctor could hardly put any more saline into it and it eventually popped and all the saline leaked into my body.

He tried it again by putting another tissue expander in my body and that one popped also, but at least this time we had enough skin to work with. I'll never forget this surgery because they did it as a day surgery and I wasn't used to having to be active right after surgery. Normally when I had surgery, I was expected to sleep all day and the next day and I wasn't allowed out of bed. With day surgery, they expect you to be up and around within hours of getting out of the operating room.

Max and my sister Kim were sitting beside me and the nurse was getting me out of bed to go to the bathroom, I could hardly walk. When I got down to where the bathroom was, I sat down on the toilet and the next thing I remember was falling, as I was reaching for the nurse's call button. The nurse came running for me, but I had fallen off the toilet and there was blood everywhere. I fainted, but as I fell, I ended up pulling out my intravenous and that's what made the blood squirt. The nurse decided to get me a wheelchair and she took me back to my bed.

Max and Kim were really worried because they saw all this blood on me. The nurse couldn't understand why I wasn't able to walk by that time and phoned my doctor. He informed her that I wasn't used to having to be mobile so quickly so they let me sleep for a few hours more before kicking me out.

*Dear Kel*

*The next summer we had to go back for more surgery. Your webbed arm had to be loosened with grafts and your other arm needed grafting to loosen more contractions. It was so hard to take you into the hospital for surgery, I was sick for days before we had to go. I just hated putting you through all the pain. You had a great attitude though and at least you weren't in the hospital for months at a time anymore.*

*I'll never forget this story. Because of your body cast and how your arms were straight out, you couldn't feed yourself so you always needed help from us to eat. You asked if I could feed you some grapes, but I was busy making supper, so I asked you to wait a minute. The next thing I saw was you eating grapes off the couch. You had lined up the grapes in a row on the couch and was eating them with your mouth. I couldn't stop laughing.*

*I have tried very hard over the years to forget all the times in the hospital, each & every time we had to go & what had to be done, but it went on for years. You had your ups & downs with it all, some good experiences, some not so good. Once in the Charles Camsell Hospital in Edmonton, you had skin grafting and a nurse decided that your donor site dressings were supposed to be changed everyday. Well I went ballistic, that was definitely a no, no. She was damaging the donor sites, we had been through this more than enough to know she was wrong. She was off of your case immediately.*

*Love MoM*

# THE GUILT

My family felt tremendous guilt over my accident, and not once did they ever deal with it as a family. It was really too bad because they could have had such peace if they would have talked about it. My accident was the taboo topic in our family. It was an unspoken rule that it was never ever to be spoken about to anyone.

My cousin Rod was only nine at the time and he felt guilty because as far as he was concerned, the spark should have landed on him, not his little two year old cousin. My other cousin Mike was 11 and he felt tremendous guilt because he threw the shingle in the fire, it was his fault I got burnt as far as he was concerned. If he wouldn't have thrown the shingle in the fire, his little cousin wouldn't have gotten burnt. My Mom also felt tremendous guilt because if she would have kept me in the house, I wouldn't have been outside watching the fire. My Dad felt tremendous guilt because he wasn't there at all. He was working out in the gym following his dream to be a world champion boxer. My Popa, felt tremendous guilt because he was the one who told them to burn the shingles. If he wouldn't have told them to burn the shingles, I never would have gotten burnt.

My Nana, felt tremendous guilt and relief. She was finally relieved of the horrible feelings that she had for me. Ever since the day I was born she had feelings that something very bad would happen to me. She just knew something would happen, but didn't know what it would be. She always thought she would back over me, so she always made my Popa back the car out of the garage. The day I got burnt, was the day she was relieved of those horrible feelings. She felt tremendous guilt because she wasn't there to protect me.

My other Nana (Nana T, my dad's Mom) was on holidays and she had been to a psychic the day before and the psychic predicted that something very horrible was going to happen to the family who had a pregnant woman – my Mom was pregnant with my sister at the time I got burnt. My Nana T blamed everyone there for my injuries, and they all felt it whether they were to blame or not.

*Dear Kel,*

*I do remember once when you were in your 20's, we were all talking over at Nana & Popa's house and your tragedy came up and Rod asked what I thought about him and Mike. I reassured him that I didn't blame him and we had this big conversation for a while. It was never their fault.*

*Popa blames himself and developed asthma from the psychological scars of it all. He could never justify why he was so stupid to have left you three kids alone doing such a dangerous thing. Nana just felt guilty, not sure for what, but remember you were her first precious granddaughter.*

*I think, now that you have your three wonderful children, you realize what a mother would do for them. There is nothing more important, nothing more cherished, or loved than your children. You see, you were my dream come true, I was afraid to even wish for a little girl when I was pregnant with you. I wanted a baby girl & I was sure that God was going to disappoint me with a boy, so we didn't even pick out any girls names. Your Dad asked me on the way to the hospital, "What if we have a girl?" and I said "We won't be that lucky, but just in case, we will call her Kelly."*

*So when Dr. Alan Day said that you were a girl I was ecstatic and that was on 9:46 am, Wednesday July 14th 1966.*

*Love, MoM*

# STARING AND TEASING

As I grew up, there was tons of staring and there still is, I just don't notice it as much anymore; in fact, people who are with me notice it more than I do. And in a way I find it funny and confusing. I live in a small city and since I've been here all my life, I feel like everyone should know me and should have seen my scars by now. There shouldn't be a need to stare at me since everyone should know my story by now.

How do I handle all the staring and teasing? In the beginning, I handled it whatever way I felt was necessary at the time. Sometimes I would just turn around so they couldn't get a second or third look, other times I would stare back and give them a dirty look, and then there were times I would just stick out my tongue at them. I hated being stared at as a kid and I have to admit, I didn't always handle it in the best way.

One time, I remember when a teenager and his sister came up to me and he was very polite and asked me if I had many plastic surgeries. I should have been nice to him, but he had caught me off guard and I basically said to him take a hike, it's none of your business. It's probably the one time I felt wrong in how I handled his question.

One time, I remember when I was in the girls' bathroom and I was wearing a one piece jumpsuit. In order to go to the bathroom, I had to take my whole outfit off. I went into the cubicle and when I was sitting there, I noticed some other girl trying to peek through the door cracks to get a look at my scars. I was really annoyed at her, and shook my head and leaned forward so she couldn't see anything. That was the last time I ever wore clothes where I had to take them all off just to go pee.

The swimming pool was the worst place for me to be stared at as I didn't let my scars stop me from wearing a bathing suit. I saw no need to hide myself just because someone else was uncomfortable with my looks. Maybe I didn't handle the staring in the best way, but I was just tired of being stared at. I was tired of people thinking I was any different than them. Because so many people were rude about my appearance, I didn't feel a need to tell everyone how I got burnt.

I'll never forget one time I was in the swimming pool change room in grade-six. We were there for school swimming lessons. A lot of the girls were changing in the common area, but a few of us wanted to change in the private cubicles. As I was going to go in to one, I heard an argument happening.

I could hear two girls saying to one of the other "ugly" girls that she wasn't allowed to change in the private cubicles because she had "nothing to hide." The one girl said to me, *"Kelly, you have scars and so you have something to hide, you can go change in the cubicle, but you, (the other ugly girl) you have nothing to hide, so you have to change out here with the rest of us."*

I remember quickly running into the cubicle and being relieved that I didn't have to change with the rest of the girls, but I felt sorry that they were picking on the other girl; she didn't deserve that kind of cruelness. I felt bad that I didn't help her, but I was just so relieved that I didn't have to get naked in front of them.

Sometimes, if people asked how I got burnt, I would tell them, but most of the time I hated talking about it. I don't know why, I just didn't feel a need to tell everyone how I got burnt. And in reality, at that age, I didn't really know. I only knew rumors; I didn't know the whole truth.

It wasn't until I was 18 and my cousin Rod and I were in the sauna, one cold winter evening, after snowmobiling that he told me. As I said, the topic of my accident was a major taboo subject in our family. Although there was tremendous guilt felt by everyone no one needed to feel guilty, because I didn't blame anyone. As far as I was concerned, it was nobody's fault that I got burnt, and I didn't hold any grudges towards anyone. I even asked my cousin Rod if he felt like I blamed him and he said that no, he never felt any sense of blame from me; he knew I loved him and didn't blame him for my challenging life.

*Dear Kel,*

*When you were finally out of your room the doctors decided that you should be walking again. By this time, you had grown and so had your feet. I think it was some time in November, before Kim was born.*

*The doctors & nurses didn't know if you were going to be able to walk, but being the little trooper that you were, they held your hand and away you went. Your old shoes didn't fit and I didn't know what to do. So I phoned "Jack & Jill's" shoe store. They recognized our name and when I told them what had happened they said they would send someone over the next morning with shoes for you.*

*So as said, the next morning a salesperson came to the hospital looking for you. The nurses took him to you and he brought boxes of shoe with him & tried them on you until he found the right size for you. Voila, new shoes.*

*I'm not sure if we had to pay for the shoes or not, but from then on we were always true blue customers of Jack & Jill's Shoes. They went out of their way to accommodate us. How nice. You, of course were so proud of your new shoes. You came running to me "Mommy, mommy look at my new shoes." I was very surprised because the salesperson came before I could get there. He was to meet me at 10:00 am and got there at 9:00 am. How wonderful people can be.*

*There was also the ice. There was no air conditioning in the hospital and you were so hot, your nurse would put a big flat pan of ice on a table with a large fan behind it & they would blow this over your little tender body to keep you comfortable. You really enjoyed it. Sometimes your body would get itchy from the healing & the heat & you would squirm around and they didn't want that, you could rub off a graft under your bandages. The bandages were big and heavy, usually on your arms, graft sites and donor sites. Sometimes you looked just like a little mummy, especially when they bandaged your head.*

*Hugs, MoM*

# SCAR-FACE

I always knew that people were talking or whispering about me behind my back, but I chose to ignore it and in many ways, it was a good thing I was so deaf. I know being deaf has really helped me to protect myself from what was being said about me.

Not too long ago, a friend of mine was telling me of how she remembers very clearly one day in elementary school. She remembers looking at me straight in the eyes and wanting to ask me how I got burnt, but she couldn't, she was too scared of hurting my feelings.

One day in grade-five I was walking by my teacher's desk and I saw a piece of paper with a circle to look like a face, with eyes, nose and mouth and then scribbles all over it. And on the top "scar-face" was written on it. That picture confirmed to me that the other kids were thinking what I thought they were. Yes, I was the ugly scar-faced girl. I knew it and so did they and nobody told me any different.

That same grade, I remember one of my friends saying to me, *"Kelly, your scars will never go away."* I was pretty upset about that, she had burst my bubble. I was still hoping for that magic day that I would wake up without scars.

# QUITTER OR NOT

I often wonder how I learned to never quit. What drove me to never give up? I failed pre-beginner swimming lessons seven times, I got bucked off my horse at least a million times, maybe more, I know I got turned down to dance at least at thousand times. So why didn't I just give up on life? What made me keep going?

My son, Cody, is a kid who likes to succeed instantly, some times he gets frustrated when he tries to do something and can't get it right the first time. One day we went swimming and in order to be able to play on the blow-up obstacle course in the swimming pool, you had to prove to the lifeguard that you could swim across the whole length of the pool.

Cody tried it once and only got about three quarters of the way there and had to be saved by the lifeguard. Cody was devastated and cried and wanted to give up. Max and I talked to him and got him motivated to try again and he did and he failed two more times.

We had a hard time trying to get him to stop crying. So then I told Max, I guess it's time to pull out *"Failed Swimming Lesson Story"* and I did. Finally, Cody was calmed down and I told him about how when I was young like him I had to take swimming lessons. My doctor wanted me to swim as much as I could because he said it would loosen my scars and hopefully stop them from contracting. Swimming would be a good form of therapy for me. He also told me that I should suck on my bottom lip and hopefully it would get smaller, not bigger (after many years of that, that didn't work).

I hated swimming for a few reasons. One reason was because my one arm was crooked and doesn't straighten, so when I swim, it just doesn't work right. That arm also gets tired very quickly and easily and doesn't have the strength that my left arm does. Swimming was difficult for me, but I kept at it because my doctor said I had to.

I also hated the swimming pool because I get stared at so much by the other swimmers. Of course people are curious about what my scars are, whether they are burns or something else. One time Max and I were sitting in a hot tub, he could see the couple beside him staring at me and whispering about me. Eventually, he got really mad and said, "Look, it's just burns not some kind of contagious skin disease." The couple got up and left the hot tub. Max didn't tell me this story until just a few days ago, as I'm sure he didn't want to hurt my feelings.

So, back to the story, I asked Cody if I ever told him the story about how I failed swimming lessons seven times. Not once or twice, but seven times! I couldn't swim the whole length of the pool because my crooked arm would get too tired and sore, so I failed every time. Eventually, on the eighth time I passed. I'm not sure if they passed me because I could finally swim the whole length of the pool or because I was too old, but the lesson of this story is, to never give up. That summer, we swam so much that my blond hair turned green!

Quitting was never an option for me. I was never allowed to quit. I still remember my Uncle Jack telling me about when my cousins fell off their bikes, he would make them get right back on and go do it again. When I was learning how to waterski, my step-dad Don did the same thing with me. Yep, you fell, now get back up and try it again and don't stop trying until you get up on those water skis.

I'll never forget the time we were in our boat with my Step-dad Don, Uncle Jack, Kim and my step-brother, Wayne. Wayne always had a fear of the water and couldn't swim well at all. He wanted to jump off the boat, but couldn't, he was being a scaredy cat and my Uncle Jack was getting frustrated with him. It didn't matter what he said, Wayne wouldn't believe him that a life jacket would help him to float. Uncle Jack threw him in the lake to prove that the life jacket would make him float and he wouldn't drown. Kim and I decided we would let Uncle Jack throw us in because it was fun, not because we were scared of the water.

It was the same when I got bucked off my horse. Too bad, I got bucked off, I just had to suck it up and get back on. The philosophy was, if you don't get back on now then you never will, so get back on now and do it until you can. Seriously, quitting was not an option, no matter how bad your ego hurt or how much pain you were in.

*Dear Kel,*

*In a previous letter I wrote about the "1-1-1" code. That was an alarm sounded throughout the hospital that a patient was in dire need of resuscitation, a life or death situation. That was the time you had your near-death experience. You were revived and alive, thank the lord. I was a wreck when I saw that on your chart because I had been around the hospital long enough to know what it meant.*

*The nurse wouldn't tell me what happened, and tried to brush it off like nothing happened. I was very thankful I saw this a long time after it really happened. The nurse said they wrote it in your chart "just in case" it happened, but it really had happened, I was scared, but grateful you were still alive.*

*You truly were a fighter. The nurses & doctors were surprised at your recovery, an adult would have taken way longer to heal from such burns, but because you were such a small child you were just the best fighter ever.*

*Love, MoM*

# GARAGE SALE

A few years ago, my husband Max and I went to a garage sale. The home owners were two senior citizens. The lady took one look at me and said, *"Couldn't they do better than that?"* I was stunned and shocked. I couldn't believe that someone could be so insensitive and it took me a minute to think of something to say. Do I be rude or do I be polite?

I certainly didn't feel that I had to be polite, as she had totally hurt my feelings, so much so that it ruined my whole day. I truly was shocked beyond belief that someone could be so ignorant. I know what she meant, but still, the way she said it was so demeaning and made me feel ugly. I am proud to say that I took the high road when I replied, *"You know what? I happen to think I look pretty damn good"* and I walked away. I didn't even give her a chance to respond.

She sure knew how to make me feel crappy, but I wasn't going to let her see that. Max and I drove away, he could see how upset I was so he said, *"Kel, she's just an old lady, she didn't mean it that way."* I said, *"She meant it how she said it."* But really, it didn't matter how she meant it, it still hurt.

Her comment was so hurtful, it made all the teasing and staring seem miniscule compared to what she said. The worst part was that she didn't have even a clue about how she made me feel. She took my power away without even knowing it. This experience made me feel truly ugly. I started to think how she was calling me ugly, but didn't even know what my scars used to look like as a kid and how much they had faded over the years. She didn't know about all the surgeries I had over the past 35-years. She had absolutely no clue what I'd gone through, and as far as she was concerned, I still didn't look good enough.

Moving past this experience was tough, but eventually I had to believe what Max said. Eventually, I pushed the hurt aside and realized that her opinion didn't need to count in my world. She wasn't a person who mattered to me. I knew tonnes of other people who thought I was beautiful and don't see my scars. I just needed to realize these people mattered to me more than she did. They were the important people in my life, not her.

Another cruel story was when I walked into a bank machine and there were two other ladies getting money before me. I could tell the one lady was just a little different and wasn't "all there." She kept turning around and staring at me and I was getting annoyed with her, I even turned around so she couldn't look at me anymore. As I was waiting my turn, she turned around and said, "Do you have Aids?" I was totally shocked and this time I didn't hold back. I gave her this disgusted look, shook my head and said, "This isn't what AIDS looks like!"

**Two staring stories that I have never forgotten in my life; the garage sale lady and the bank machine lady, the other million or two I've forgotten.**

# PERFECTION

*"Just because you aren't perfect, it doesn't mean you aren't beautiful."--- Kelly*

Seriously, is there someone out there who thinks they have the perfect body, with nothing they would change? And really, does it matter if you have a perfect body?

Sure, I would love to lose those last 20 pounds and be a size zero again, but seriously, am I going to do it? Nope. Why not? Because there are other things that are more important in my life than making sure I have the perfect skinny scarless body.

I am far from having the perfect body, but I am learning to love it slowly but surely. I have a burnt ear, which I call my little ear; that I love. There was a time I didn't like it, but I have learned to love it because it is what makes me, ME.

At one time, I decided I wanted to have a prosthetic ear made but then decided against it for two reasons. Firstly, it meant cutting off my little ear and replacing it with a hand-made ear that would look like my other ear, but would it really? They said it would, but, what if I didn't like it? If I didn't like my new ear, I would have lost my old ear and there would be no way to get it back.

Sure, when other people looked at me they wouldn't see my deformed ear any more, but in reality, it really didn't bother me. I really didn't care what people thought when they saw my little deformed ear. If it made them uncomfortable, they didn't have to look.

Getting the new ear would have consisted of multiple surgeries. One surgery would have been required to cut off my current deformed ear; then another surgery would have been required to implant the titanium posts into my skull. Then I would have had to wait six weeks for the titanium posts to heal into my skull. Then they would have had to make a mold of my current ear. Then they would have had to make the new ear. I'm not sure how long that would have taken, but it could have been up to six months. Then once the ear was ready I'd finally be able to snap it on to the posts that were in my head. It seemed like a very long process just to look good for someone else to feel better, as I wasn't doing it for me. And, the other thing was, the prosthetic ear would wear out over time and I would have to get a new one made every few years or so. That's a whole lot of ears over my lifetime....

The other reason I decided against it was because Max said, *"Kel, I really don't want to nibble on a plastic ear,"* and although he would have supported me no matter what, I had to take his opinion into consideration. Now when he nibbles on my ears, I can enjoy all the sensation.

Was it really worth all the surgeries when having the new ear wasn't going to help me hear any better? Yes, it would have looked better to someone looking at me, but what if I would have forgotten to put my ear on in the morning? Then people would have been looking at a hole instead. I decided not to go ahead with getting a new ear and keep my little ear that I loved so much. I decided I couldn't live with the change. I wanted to keep my little ear I grew up with.

At one time I also thought, to improve my beauty, I should get a new nipple made. I had heard how they cut your skin in a certain way and then fold it back and stitch it together to create the nipple, and then to create the color you would get a tattoo to make it look more real. What about the other nipple? Would it look the same? Would it have any feeling? The doctor said it wouldn't. It wouldn't look totally the same and it wouldn't have any feeling.

Again, since Max is a big factor in this decision too, I asked his opinion and then spent time soul searching. Max was totally supportive and ultimately it was my decision. I told him he should just give me his nipples, but he said no to that. If it wasn't going to give me any feeling and it wasn't going to look the same as the other one, then what was the point? Was it worth another surgery, and possibly not even look as good?

My Nana used to say, "Kelly, look at those little leaves in your cheeks, your scars look like beautiful little leaves." I used to shake my head when my Nana would say that. She also used to rub lamb oil on my bald spot, she was determined to make my hair grow back, but it never did.

I love my nose. I have a bit of scarring on my nose, but otherwise, I love it. I think my nose is cute and little. I also love my green eyes. My one friend said he loved my eyes because they look so inquisitive. Hmmm, never heard that one before, but I'll take that as a compliment.

One part of my body that I hate is my lips. I have always thought I had big lips and hated them. Part of the reason I hate them is because some of the scarring makes it difficult to determine where my bottom lip ends.

Hating a body part doesn't mean that I hate ME and what I look like; I just hate one small part. I always concentrate on the features that I love about my body, my eyes, my nose, my hot ass and then I forget about my lips. I also used to hate my smile, but that didn't stop me from smiling. I knew I couldn't do that – I love life so I'm going to smile anyways.

Smiling is another great way to show how happy and beautiful you are. When people see you smile, you seem more approachable to them. So, even though I don't like my smile, I still smile because it makes me feel good. I even smile at people I don't know. A simple little smile can make someone feel so great and make their day better. Smile!

# Would I change things if I could?

One evening, I was asked to speak alongside my friend and fellow speaker, Michelle Peavy. Michelle speaks about her journey as a fearless woman. Anyways, I don't want to go into that story, what I want to talk about is the other amazing woman who spoke at her event, I don't remember her name, but she was blind and hearing-impaired. She told us of her incredible story about being a successful career woman who gradually turned blind at 38. I was so impressed at how she embraced her challenge and turned it into a life-changing positive journey.

But this is what I remembered most about her and I thought this was the most profound thing I heard all night. She was asked if she had one wish, what would it be? And of course, naturally everyone would think she would want her sight back right? NOPE! She wants to be given the gift of song! Can you believe it? How amazing is that? Other people would want their sight back, but no way, she wants to be a singer and sing alongside my friend Michelle Peavy, I was floored and of course it got me thinking too.

If I could have one wish - would I wish my scars to be gone? Hmmm, very good question, I need to think about that one - maybe as a kid, yes I would have wished my scars to be gone, but now? NOPE, no way! My scars are my gift, they make me ME and the way I'm inspiring others to find their true beauty from within. If I didn't have scars, how would I do that? My scars have been the reason I have been meeting so many amazing people who have recognized my gift and have encouraged me to tell my story. Over this past week I have seen women cry about my story and then laugh their heads off at another story of mine because they realize that I don't let my scars bring me down. I use my scars to bring happiness to my life and to enhance me and now of course others' lives.

Who else do you know could say how cute they look with pig tails in their hair at 43-years old even with their bald spot showing in the back of their head? I did it. I put in the pig tails and said to myself, *"Wow, you look cute!"* I went downstairs and Max said, *"You know, your bald spot is showing? Do you really have to wear the pig tails?"* and I said, *"Yep, so what if my bald spot is showing, I look and feel cute and I'm keeping them in."* I also said to him, *"Do you think someone is going to come up to me and say, hey lady your bald spot is showing?"* Nope, no way is anyone going to say something to me and if they're going to stare, again, SO WHAT? I've dealt with staring all my life and it's not going to stop now, so I might as well look cute and feel it and to heck with them. I don't care if they like what I look like or not. If they don't like my bald spot showing, they can just turn away. I walked out the door with the pig tails because I felt great and didn't care that my bald spot was showing.

So, the next day when I was planning my "beauty exercise" and writing in my "You're Beautiful because..." book, I asked Max, *"Ok, why do you think I'm beautiful?"* And he said, *"Because you don't give a crap what people think about what you look like and you don't let your scars stop you from doing what you want to do."* Aww, I know he was referring to the pig tails and waterpark incident. Good enough for me!

*Dear Kel,*

*I cannot sleep so I have to write more. Sorry, these things are coming to me and I have to write them down so I don't forget again. You realize that your name – Kelly- means "fighter", needless to say when we named you Kelly that you would be truly in for the fight of your life.*

*The night you were burned, when the doctors had you in the operating room, they opened your right arm, with a slash that went from your wrist to your elbow. This was to stop your arm from bursting from all the body fluids that were rushing there to cool the burns, they were very deep.*

*Once when they were debriding you in the operating room, Dr. Brown, a plastics resident with Dr. Shimizu was cleaning the burned skin off your right ear. He did not know it until it was gone, but he took off the top of your ear. That's how you got your little ear. It was just the curl that came off but as it healed, the scar tissue contracted drawing the ear in. A couple of years later Dr. Shimizu tried to repair it with a graft, but the same contraction happened again and he decided that using your skin on your ear was not a good idea and wasteful of the limited skin you had.*

*Remember Kel, you were a very happy child and you enjoyed company and we played as much as we could with you to pass the time in the hospital. We sang songs, such as "Jesus Loves Me This I Know" and all the other little songs that we sang. We read books to you and we were happy. Remember, I am a Pisces & I do not like reality and so it is easy for me to pretend things are not as they seem. The words to the song are as follows:*

*"MY SPECIAL ANGEL"*

*You are my precious angel, sent from up above. The Lord smiled down on me & sent an angel to love. You are my special angel, right from paradise, I know that you're an angel, heaven's in your eyes. A smile from your lips brings the summer sunshine, the tears from your eyes bring the rain, I feel your touch your warm embrace and I'm in heaven again. You are my special angel through eternity, I'll have my special angel here to watch over me.*

*Love MoM*

# PREGNANCIES

Many people asked me what it was like being pregnant as a burn survivor. Before I got pregnant, my biggest question was whether I could even have a baby. I was also concerned with whether my scars would stretch enough. If everything went well, I also questioned if I would produce milk or not.

The answer to all of the questions was YES. Yes, I was able to get pregnant, yes my scars stretched enough and yes, I produced milk.

It was pretty crazy shortly after I had my daughter Alexanna, as a few days later I felt a little wetness on my breast and looked down and sure enough, my little thing I call a nipple, actually did have holes and the milk leaked.

I was shocked. The irony was that I don't wear a bra, so how the heck was I going to wear one of those nipple pads that I got from the Welcome Wagon baby gift? Yikes! And even still, what was going to happen with the other breast that didn't have a nipple?

I wore a really tight tank top that was too small for me. Tight enough that it held the nipple pad in place, plus gave me enough tightness to help the engorgement go down. Yes, I was in pain for a few weeks, but eventually it all went away.

We were really quite concerned about my scars when I was pregnant with the twins. I had gained all the weight right in my belly. I had 12-ultrasounds throughout the pregnancy, my doctor wanted to make sure that the twins were growing at an even weight. The twins were taking everything I had, and actually caused me to lose weight one month. My scars were extremely tight and eventually tore. The tears were like little paper cuts that bled a tiny little bit.

At about 29-weeks I began leaking amniotic fluid and I thought my water had broken so I went into the hospital. My doctor was concerned that twin B's sack had broke, but not twin A's. Twin A is the twin that is closest to the cervix and would come first. They thought that twin A was blocking the passage, therefore stopping the leaking from twin B. They did an ultrasound, and eventually determined that this wasn't the case and the twins were all good. My doctor chose to give me steroids to help develop the twins' lungs just in case I went into early labour. They were quite impressed that I made it to 29-weeks and hoped I would get as close as possible to 40-weeks before delivering them.

I'll never forget when the peri-natal doctor came to visit me. He was trying to convince me to breast feed the twins. He kept telling me how important it was and I kept telling him how impossible it was going to be with one partial nipple. He told me again how I really should consider it and I told him again only louder how impossible it was going to be to feed two starving babies with one partial nipple. Not one, but two babies, with just one nipple. I don't think he understood the mechanics of it. I was pretty sure that to feed two babies, I should have two complete nipples! And the nipple I did have, was so tiny, there would be no way a baby could latch on to it. Let's just say, I'm happy I won that battle. Millions of bottles was way easier than trying to feed two starving babies with one partial nipple. Plus everyone else could help me feed them too.

When I was about 32-weeks pregnant, I was four pounds shy of 200 and about 70" around, and I could barely walk 20-feet without needing to have a break. I was exhausted from being pregnant and my scars felt so extremely tight that it seemed I would burst at any time. Max used to tease me and call me rolly-polly and when we tried to pass each other down the hall, he would have to back up and let me through first because we couldn't fit through together.

I finally convinced my doctor that he should think about inducing me, as I couldn't take the tightness any more. I also had major heart burn and was taking medication for that as well. He decided to do an amniocentesis on me to check on the twins' lungs and make sure they were developed enough. They were, so he said *"Ok let's get these twins induced."* The next day I was in the hospital delivering the twins.

We didn't have boy names picked out, only girl names. Max bought a baby name book and as we were waiting for the medication to kick-in, we started scrambling.

Eventually after 30-hours of labour and an emergency caesarian section, the twins came and we didn't know what to call them. Finally, the nurse said to us, *"Look, you have to name these babies, we can't keep calling them twin A and twin B."* I just laughed, why couldn't I? I'll never forget when the recovery nurse asked me how I was feeling. I said *"Great, I don't have any heart burn and my scars aren't so tight."* I think she thought I was a little bit weird, but she didn't know what it felt like to have scars tight as could be and carrying two babies.

After two days, they were named Cody Allen (his middle name was my step-dad's middle name) and Parker David (his middle name was my Dad's middle name). Cody was 6 pounds, 11 ounces and Parker was 6 pounds, 7 ounces.

Once the doctor told me the boys were here, I wanted, more than anything, to know how big they were. How was a little thing like me able to grow such big babies and still deliver three and a half weeks early? For some reason, I don't feel sorry for women who are pregnant with just one baby – just kidding.

# ANGEL BABY ALEISHA

In between Alexanna and the twins, I was pregnant a second time. This pregnancy did not go as well. I delivered a stillborn at 28-weeks. This experience was the absolute worst time of my life. I lost my baby and totally blamed myself. She was inside me; it had to be my fault; nobody else could have caused her to die.

We called in my pastor, Pastor Morck and he came to the hospital to bless our baby and perform a naming ceremony, we named her Aleisha. My Aunt Diane crocheted her a tiny little white baptism gown, it was beautiful and made our little angel baby look gorgeous.

The nurses took hand prints, foot prints and pictures of her so that when we were ready to look at them, we would have them. The nurses were so incredibly compassionate and loving; they truly understood how difficult it was to deliver a stillborn and go home with empty arms. I even wrote a letter to the president of the hospital to make sure those specific nurses got recognized.

I was really glad when my doctor had insisted on an autopsy so that we could confirm what happened to her. My doctor told me that where the umbilical cord is connected to the baby, it grew shut instead of open. She wasn't getting any nutrients from me and therefore she passed on. Although I was extremely upset about losing our baby daughter, I was glad that I knew what happened to her. I knew it wasn't my fault anymore and it helped to relieve my pain.

Ultimately, I realized that Aleisha's death was a gift, a gift to us on earth and a gift to our families in heaven. If she had been born, we wouldn't have had her twin brothers, we would have stopped at her and only had two girls.

One of my longtime, dearest friends Rhonda had a very similar experience happen to her. Rhonda and I have a very unique situation. We go back four generations; our great-grandparents were friends, then our parents, then us, and now our kids are friends. Her grandma is Bertha Schumm, my Auntie Bertie who couldn't stay away from the hospital and waved at me every day. She was also at our house the day I got home from the hospital back in 1968.

I always felt so bad when Rhonda lost her angel baby, Angelica because I didn't understand what she was going through. I didn't understand doing the naming ceremony or the pictures or the memorial. I didn't get it at all, and I felt like I didn't show Rhonda enough compassion. It wasn't until we lost our baby that I truly understood what she went through. Although it was the worst thing in the world that we both had to go through, it was also another thing that tied us together as the great friends we are.

*Dear Kel,*

*I have to tell you this story just in case I don't remember later. They had a parents' room on the station where all the parents could gather and visit with family & friends. Well, this one day I was sitting there and saw a little boy being pushed in a stroller by an older lady about 40. Her little boy was four years old and had bruises all over his body. I thought how terrible, she beats her child and there she is pushing him around like nothing happened.*

*Later, after talking with the lady I found out that her son, named Kenny, had Leukemia. The doctor discovered it when he was two years old. Now Kenny was four and he was in stage four of the disease and was going to die. They were trying all kinds of experimental drugs on Kenny, but none of them worked.*

*A short while later Kenny passed on to heaven and thanks to Kenny there are children living because of him. I had to suck it up, my horrible thought about such a nice lady. She was losing her wonderful son and at such a young age. How terrible. I started to be grateful, you were on the mend and you were going to live a long & happy life, you were going to live. All that was going to happen to you is that you were going to have some scars. Big deal, we still had you.*

*Your doctor, Dr. Shimizu also offered us a challenge, that if we tried to hide you away from the public eye, places or things such as school etc, that he would not think twice of having you taken away from us and raised normally. That was quite a challenge, but by this time there was no problem for us. You were normal as far as we were concerned, you just had scars, but inside you would always be our beautiful little girl. I know I never said that out loud to you because that would have been giving you a big head and made you vain. Now I know that was wrong but that's the way we were raised. Nana always said it was better to have people compliment you rather than brag about yourself & prove yourself wrong.*

*Kel you were a normal kid with a normal sister. You taught Kim everything you knew. You were a very good big sister. You would show her all the things you knew and how to do things, like ride a tricycle, go on a sled, make snow angels. You also taught Kim to use the pottie at only 17-months old. The two of you were very happy children, loving and kind.*

*Love, MoM*

# BURN CAMP AND BURN CONFERENCES

I believe there is tremendous power in knowing other people like you who have been through similar experiences in life. I didn't realize what that power was like until I went to my first World Burn Congress in Edmonton, a gazillion years ago. When I attended that conference and met other people who could talk about similar experiences and challenges, and share the same language, I realized what I was missing out on.

I'll never forget when I met my friend Cindy Rutter at my first World Burn Congress. She also got burnt as a child and so we hit it off instantly. We both had been through many of the same experiences growing up with scars. What I remember most is talking to her about having kids. I just assumed that since I was burnt there was no way I could have kids. She told me how she had kids and so did many other women burn survivors. She was my inspiration to get pregnant.

Burn camp is similar, but for kids, which is so awesome. I wish there would have been a burn camp when I was young, I know meeting other kids like me would have given me more courage to keep on persevering in life. It would have given me someone else to talk to about boys, relationships, the staring and teasing.

When I was growing up, I thought I was the only burnt person in the whole world. I didn't know anybody else like me. One day I had a conversation with my Mom and I said,

> *"Mom, I'm the only burnt person in the whole world?"* She replied, *"No, you aren't."*

> *"Well, then I'm the only burnt person in all of Canada?"* Again she replied, *"No, you aren't."*

> *"Well, then I'm the only burnt person in all of Alberta?"* Patiently she replied, *"No, you aren't."*

*"Well then in Edmonton – I MUST be the only burnt person in Edmonton." She said, "Well, ok you might be."*

I think my Mom just wanted to shut me up, but truly, I didn't meet another burnt person until I was 18, and wow, he freaked me out! I didn't know what to think, and I remember saying to myself, this is what another burnt person looks like? He doesn't look like me.

I have been very fortunate to be chosen to attend the Children's Burn Camp in Taiwan. The Canadian Burn Foundation chose Max and I to go there and chaperone five Canadian kids. What an amazing experience.

Not only did we get to go to the Taiwan Children's Burn Camp, but we got to go to their hospital and visit the burn unit. What I found so fascinating about being at burn camp in Taiwan was that there were so many kids just like ours who were burnt and on the other side of the world. See, I wasn't the only one burnt in the whole world, I guess my Mom was right after all.

One time Max and I got invited to go to the Children's Burn Camp in Chicago. The firefighters were putting on this amazing carnival for all the kids. Every kid won at least 10 stuffed animals of all sizes. Some of the bears were bigger than the kids, and they could hardly carry them. We were invited to go because one of our friends was invited to entertain the kids there with balloon animals and Max was an entertainer too.

I'll never forget a conversation I had with one of the firefighters there. While we were talking, I saw a little boy in a wheelchair who was recently burnt, and had just been released from the hospital. He was a 100% burn and his legs had been burned off to his knees, both arms burned off to his elbows and he was covered in bandages from head to toe.

I was touched and very sad when I saw him. I asked the firefighter, what happened to him and he said, his parents used him as a human sacrifice and he survived. I was SHOCKED! I could not believe that parents could do something so cruel. I was hoping that his parents were burned alive. That was the ultimate worst burn injury story that I ever heard in my life, and I was devastated. Suddenly, after hearing that, I realized how lucky and grateful I was to have such great parents, family and friends.

Burn camp is also the one week where burn kids can go and not be stared at or teased. It is the week when they can truly relax and not worry about the risk of being hurt, whether it is emotionally or physically.

One time I had a conversation with a physiotherapist at burn camp. I was a little confused, I thought our burn camp was going to be just for burn kids, but we didn't have enough kids to fill the camp so we had to share it with other non-burn kids. I remember seeing all the non-burn kids at the entranceway, there were about 10 of them and then I saw one of our burn kids walking through the group and going through the door; I could feel his tension and pain.

I knew what that kid was feeling. I knew what it was like to walk through a group of non-burn kids and know that you're being stared at and judged, will probably be whispered about when you're past them; or maybe not even past them. They might start whispering about you as you're walking by.

The physiotherapist was giving me a really rough time about an issue, although I can't remember what it was about now. I was telling her how I had really hoped that burn camp would be just burn kids and their siblings. She was really upsetting me and I got mad and I said, *"Look, you have absolutely no clue what it is like to walk through a group of people and be stared at because you're ugly."*

She didn't know what to say, because I was right, but even when I said it, she still didn't understand. She's a beautiful woman who loves to be on display. She loves the attention and has absolutely no clue what it's like to be stared at for all the crappy reasons. I told her that burn camp is supposed to be the one week of the year that a burn kid is supposed to feel totally secure and not have to worry about staring and teasing. This camp did not accomplish that mission that year, as far as I was concerned.

*Dear Kel,*

*The nurses asked if you were baptized and what religion we were so that a parson could come and visit. The people at our church were praying for you, all our friends and family everywhere were praying. You just had to live. I could not go on without you. That would be just too hard. You were too much of our lives, too precious, too dear. We all love you so very much. People always said what a beautiful little girl you were, so cute. You had those wonderful eyes that you still have. They have always been so special, so beautiful. Please God do not take our baby from us.*

*The University of Alberta Hospital was and still is a teaching hospital; therefore every day there were interns, residents and nurses coming in to your room to see you and your burns. Not very many people survived with such extensive burns back then. No one so young had ever been so badly burned and lived; you were a miracle.*

*They would gown up and come into your room and touch you and look at you like you were some kind of special case. I noticed that this really upset you & your temperature would rise and it was not good for you. I remember discussing this with your nurse and she said to talk to Dr. Shimizu and get it stopped. That's exactly what we did, but you still got a very serious infection in your tiny little body and it was going to kill you. The lab technicians and doctors couldn't find a drug to cure your infection. Finally, after a week they found an antibiotic that would stop the infection and you were on the mend, but during that time you had a "1-1-1" code.*

*I noticed it on your chart one night. A 1-1-1 code is a near death experience and you were still in serious trouble. You were going to die, but thanks to the doctors & nurses again, they revived you. I just about died myself when I saw this on your chart, because this was a while into your recovery – like within the first month that this happened and I thought we were in the clear. I didn't realize that there was still a chance that you could die.*

*Love, MoM*

# SOCIAL MEDIA

What I love about social media and technology is that people today are able to keep in better contact now than ever. When I was speaking to the 4-H kids at Club Week, I told them how lucky they were that they would be able to develop these great friendships and keep them forever because of social media.

While I was speaking to them I asked them, *"Who in here likes to text?"* Every single one of them put up their hand. *"Who is on Facebook?"* Every single one of them put up their hand again. I just laughed and said, *"Hey guys, I'm all over that, it is so awesome that you will be able to stay connected in the world with people who have similar interests as you."*

In today's world, it is all about social networking and developing friendships and relationships. The world is so connected; now more than ever.

Most of my friends are on Facebook, and I love this because I interact way more now with my friends and family than ever before. Facebook is a great way to show your friends and family your pictures, videos and just to communicate on a daily basis. I am so happy that my cousins from around the world contact me now where we didn't before. It wasn't because we didn't love each other, it was because life is so busy, that we didn't take the time to write a letter, phone or even physically get together.

What I also love is that I have been able to meet other burn survivors, like me, on Facebook. The neatest part is the uniqueness of each person. Every burn survivor has a different story, with nobody's story being the same. Some people were burnt because of car accidents, a house fire or a work injury. Others were burnt because they poured gasoline all over themselves and wanted to commit suicide, but their worst nightmare comes true and they end up living, having to face the rest of their life with another issue. Everybody's story is different, and it is great that we have ways to connect each other and share stories and help us through our traumatic events.

Following is a Facebook email my cousin Robbie sent me just before my model search event:

**Rob** March 20 at 5:24am

I don't say this enough to you, but I am so very proud of you. I always have been. I tell everyone in my life about you and how tough you are. I don't remember if I ever told you, but I cut off all my hair for you. I donated it to a non-profit that makes wigs for little girls who are burn victims or cancer survivors. I love you very much.

Don't forget to knock them all dead!

**Kelly** March 22 at 9:00am

Hey Rob - It warms my heart tremendously to hear your words. I know we don't get to tell each other often enough how much we mean to each other, but that is what's so great about Facebook, we've been in way better contact now than ever before and I love that! No, you didn't tell me about your hair and I think that is so awesome! I'm sure the little girl is so happy to have your hair and she would be proud to wear it. I'm sure her self esteem has been lifted tremendously because of your contribution.

I love you very much too cuz! And I can't wait to see you in Aug! I did the best I could and won the People's Choice award. Like my one friend said on my status (she's a burn survivor also), the people are smarter than the judges. lol.

I am so glad this is over with and I can go back to being my authentic self, this modeling stuff is definitely not for me! First thing I did when I got to my cuzn's place was took off the makeup. We stayed the night at my cuzn's rod's house - he's my cuzn who was with me when I got burnt.

Take care and keep in touch! Luv ya! kel

# BEAUTY

*"I have learned to love my scars & know they make me different & beautiful. Only I can make me feel beautiful not others." -- Kelly*

## The Ugly Girl

When I was in elementary school, I learned from a very young age who was "pretty" and who wasn't. I always wanted to be considered one of the pretty girls, but I knew that the reality was: I wasn't. I still remember in grade-six when one of the guys said that there were only three girls in our class who hadn't been kissed yet, and I was one of those girls. He made it very clear that I was one of the chosen "three" who none of the boys wanted to kiss.

When I was young, and since I was labeled as one of the "ugly" girls, I also felt that I didn't deserve to look good or feel good. I put this wall up around myself and thought that since I was "ugly" I shouldn't even think about dressing like any of the "pretty" girls. It wasn't until late junior high/early senior high that I realized that I deserved to look and feel good! I started babysitting and earning money so I could save up to buy clothes. I no longer wanted to wear my Nana's hand-made clothes any more. I wanted to wear store bought jeans and t-shirts like all the pretty girls were wearing. My best friend at the time would take me shopping and help me to buy clothes that looked great on me and I learned to feel great about what I looked like.

But here's what I know – school is only one phase of life. It can be the most cruel and toughest thing you can ever face, but once you get through it, the world of possibilities opens up and life gets better. I know it's very tough to endure 12-years of teasing, put-downs, and told that you're not good enough; and then somehow when you get out of school, you have to feel great and beautiful. It was tough, and it took me a lot of years to finally accept that beauty truly does come from within.

I was preparing for my keynote about the "Beauty from Within" for a group of Aboriginal women at their "Women Empowering Women" conference and one of the things I made was a beauty book. I put on the cover, "I am beautiful because...." The inside cover has a list of reasons I feel I am beautiful. In order to get the content for the book, I did some soul searching about myself, and then I asked my first boyfriend, a couple other guys who I knew had a crush on me, and then Max why I was beautiful to them. My first boyfriend said that he was attracted to me because of my laugh. He thought I had a great sense of humor and he loved how much we laughed together. He said at times he thought I was going to pass out from laughing so much, and he's never met another woman who laughed as much as me.

My elementary school crush, said it was because I shared cookies with him. He said I shared cookies with him every day from kindergarten to grade-five. I just laughed when he told me that. Well, I thought he was the cutest boy in the whole school, why wouldn't I share my cookies with him? I suppose my Nana and Mom were right, as they always taught me the way to a boy's heart is through his stomach.

So what does beauty mean to me, and what makes me feel beautiful? Like you, I've heard the phrase *"beauty is in the eyes of the beholder"* and yes, that is true, but I just hate that phrase because it's so lame. One of my best friends told me that he feels beauty is something you feel with all your senses. Wow, I like that one.

To me, beauty is whatever makes you feel great. For example, one day I wore a pair of jeans to work. I love these jeans; I call them my "hot ass" jeans because I love how my ass looks in them. Yep, and I'm not afraid to say it. I wore the jeans to work paired with sandals. I thought I looked good, and I felt good, but not near as good as I felt when I put my black heels on. When I put my heels on and started walking around, all of a sudden, I went, *"Wow, I feel sexy!"* My second thought was what just happened here? I was wearing sandals and felt good, but when I put my heels on, something magical happened in my head and I felt great. Hey, I have to remember this – I feel great wearing jeans with heels and absolutely have to do this more often! I loved the fact that I recognized something that made me feel beautiful and sexy.

Another thing that makes me feel beautiful is nice nails. It never used to phase me until I had my nails done, and then realized how great a person's hands looked when their nails were manicured. I started wearing fake nails so that my hands looked great, and then I felt another wow! All these little things that I'm working on are changing me and making me feel so awesome.

Ok, so what else makes me feel great? This one is BIG and something that everyone needs more of and something that I talked to the ladies about in my keynote. COMPLIMENTS!

Yes, compliments. Do you recognize how great you feel when someone gives you a compliment? Most people try to brush them off with an *"Oh yeah right, whatever. Sure, I'm wearing a nice dress, but it's old and really doesn't deserve to be complimented."* Stop right there! In order to feel great, you need to accept and receive the compliments.

I love compliments and I've learned that most people only share a compliment when they truly mean it. I know I do, and I try to make it a rule that I compliment someone each day. I don't care if it's someone I know or don't know, I want people to feel great about themselves. I have no problem, when I'm in the elevator with someone and they're wearing a fabulous outfit and they look great, telling them that they truly do look good. Why not?

Why not give a compliment? I believe that life is too full of negatives and that people need to feel like they're doing something right in life and what better way than to take 30-seconds out of your life and to say, *"Hey, you look great!"*

You see, something else I believed in was that there was a beauty scale and everyone fits into certain categories and there's only room for so many people in each category. For example, there are the ugly-looking people, homely-looking people, ok-looking people, good-looking people, beautiful-looking people, gorgeous-looking people, drop-dead gorgeous-looking people, sexy-looking people and stunning-looking people.

I always thought I was at the bottom of the scale and everyone else was above me. Now I believe something totally different. I got rid of my stupid belief of there being a "beauty scale." I believe that anyone can be beautiful as long as they believe they are. I also believe that there can be tonnes of beautiful or drop dead gorgeous people in this world. I also believe that it really doesn't matter what anyone else thinks. It only matters what YOU think and what you perceive yourself to believe and what gives you that inner feeling of greatness.

When I was speaking at the Women Empowering Women conference, I performed my "Beauty Exercise." I had the girls help me make a list on the flip chart and put up the most common beauty words that people use to describe people. Some of the common words are stunning, beautiful, sexy, hot, gorgeous, a "10", good looking, etc. Then I had the girls pick one word that describes them. I knew they'd be uncomfortable because most people think they're at the bottom of the pile, not the top so I said to the girls, *"Ok, you may not think that you're one of those words, and if you asked me a few years ago, my word wasn't on that list at all. I didn't think I was beautiful or gorgeous or fabulous, but guess what – I've had guys call me that now and I'm over 40."*

I never got those compliments when I was a kid and desperately seeking them; I get them now because the boundaries are gone and the guys/men aren't scared to dish out compliments because there's nobody judging them now. I also don't see the compliments as flirting, I see them as compliments and I'm going to take as many of them as I can get!

And finally, I believe that in order to receive a compliment, you need to give them. I love getting compliments because they make me feel great.

## Who do I look like?

When we finally decided to have kids, I always wanted a daughter. I was so glad I had her first because I was so proud to be one of the moms who got the daughter she always wanted.

I wanted a daughter for a couple reasons, one because I thought raising a girl would be easier since I am one and secondly because secretly I wanted to know who she was going to look like.

As I was growing up, I always wanted to know what I would look like without scars. I used to look at myself in the mirror and try to imagine what I would look like without scars and I would wonder if I'd be beautiful if I didn't have my scars?

One time when I was a very young kid, I wondered if my daughter would be born with scars on her face. I told Max the story and he said, *"Nope, she's not going to have scars on her face because she's going to look like me."* I just laughed at him. She does have his freckles, but she has my Mom's big brown eyes.

When I was interviewed by a local television station, the interviewer asked me whether I had learned anything from my daughter and I said, *"I'm not sure what I've learned from her, but here's what I wonder: I wonder if she is who I would have looked like if I didn't have scars."*

When I said that, I could see his eyes light up. Yes, that is a thought I've had many times. Would I look like my daughter if I didn't have scars?

One of my friends, Cindy Rutter, who is also a burn survivor and the one who encouraged me to have kids, talked about who we would look like without scars. I asked her if, when she was growing up, if she wondered what she would look like without scars. She said yes, she did and then she told me that her daughter looks exactly like her. I thought that her knowing this was so amazing. I told her how I hoped my daughter would look like me so I would know what I looked like and instead of scars, but she has beautiful freckles.

## Feeling Fabulous

Why is it that when the runway coach (more about the model search later in the book) was telling me I was fabulous, it didn't make me feel fabulous? Even though he told me a hundred times? How come he couldn't convince me he was telling the truth?

Very interesting thought and here's what I came up with. Ben Barry tweeted, *"How have you defined beauty in your own terms and challenged the status quo notion today?"* I became the blabber mouth that day - it took three tweets to say what I had to say. The three things I said were:

1) I define beauty as being the best YOU, you can be and following your dreams and passions in life. Beauty is about U and U only.

2) I have learned to love my scars & know they make me different & beautiful. Only I can make me feel beautiful not others.

3) I challenged the status quo by entering the "Every Woman" Competition as a burn survivor and won the People's Choice Award.

The cool thing about my response, was that Ben re-tweeted the second message. If you're new to the twitter world, this means that he wanted his followers to hear what I had to say and posted it for them to see. It is an honour when someone re-tweets what you say, so I was really excited about it because that also meant that he thought it was good.

This re-tweet also got me thinking, why is it that people can tell you you're beautiful or fabulous like the runway coach did and you don't feel it? My answer was *"it's because only I can make me feel beautiful not others. True beauty is all in the head and if your head doesn't believe it, neither will you."*

Yes, that's right - true beauty is all in the head. Why is it that when we see a beautiful, drop-dead gorgeous woman, if you ask her if she thinks she's beautiful she might say no? Hmmm, not all of them will say no, but a good majority of women will say they don't think they're beautiful. And then on the flip side, how come if you ask a person who you think is not good looking the same question, she may say she feels beautiful? Hmmm, another one to think about.

Here's what I know, true inner beauty comes from your head. It's your head that tells you what to feel. Some days I feel totally ugly and crappy and there's nothing anyone can say or do to make me feel better. And then there's the days when I wake up, do my hair and I just feel great. Sometimes I even feel greater than great and there's nothing any one can say to drop me down a notch. It's all in the head. True beauty is all in your head and what you think about is what you feel. If you keep telling your brain that you "feel" ugly, then eventually your brain believes it and vice versa.

There was no way that when the runway coach told me I looked fabulous that I felt fabulous because my head was telling me he was full of crap. My reason for thinking this was because I was doing something that was not authentic to me. I didn't feel like I was being my authentic self by walking that runway and having everyone stare at me for being a model.

As I grew up, I had a very different opinion of models than most. As a kid, I envied and loathed models because they had something I didn't. They had beautiful outer looks that could attract any guy they wanted. I didn't have that. I had to find other ways to attract guys and it wasn't until I got out of high school that guys felt more secure letting down their boundaries and admitting they had feelings for me. I wasn't the girl that the guys were drooling over.

Yes, I had a very bad attitude towards models when I was growing up. I am glad that I walked in their shoes and have realized how challenging and brave it is to be a model. I am also glad that I don't have that opinion of models any more and that I have found my own true beauty too.

It was when I was up on the runway and speaking and answering the judge's questions that I felt beautiful, and you know why? Because I was being my authentic self - I loved the speaking and sharing of my message with the audience. Now if the runway coach would have told me I was fabulous at that moment, I would have believed him. It's all in the head, and if you are following your passion and being your authentic self you will feel beautiful.

*Dear Kel,*

*When it was finally time to let you out of your room, one of the nurses had an old carriage stroller. They put blankets and pillows in it so that we were able to load you into the stroller and take you out of your room. This was November the 16th, 1968 a Saturday, I remember this because it was the day before your sister Kim was born. You were so happy to see something other than the four walls in your room.*

*Well Kel, we walked the halls of that hospital, we must have gone about 100 miles. At least that's what it felt like to me. Every time I wanted to stop, you wanted to go. "Mommy please, let's go again?" So off we'd go again. I was very glad when your Dad arrived because I gave him the job.*

*The next morning at 9 am, we were going to go to visit you, but I had back pain. I called Dr. Ringham and he said I should stay home, so off your Dad went to spend the day with you. Up & down the halls, the two of you went. When he returned at 9 pm, the back pain was not better, even worse. I called the doctor & three hours later Kim Sue was born. I was the only woman in maternity at the hospital so Kim got the best care ever. All those nurses and one baby, spoiled or what?*

*I got caught up on my rest and spent 10-days in the hospital and when I returned to the hospital I was back at my fighting weight. 140 lbs. Svelte and ready. Your poor Dad, had a heck of a time, he would go to work, then go see you and end his evening by visiting me in the other hospital.*

*Finally when I got out of the hospital, I was walking down the hall towards the children's play area and you were in there along with all the other kids on station 34 and when you saw me, you came running. I dropped to my knees so you could come into my arms and we had a huge long hug. I scooped you up into my arms & didn't let you go for a very long time.*

*After a while we went to visit the nursery & I showed you the babies. I told you that we had a baby girl just like that for you at home. You were very excited. More later.*

*Love MoM*

## PART TWO – What makes me tick and motivates ME

Part two was written because people are always asking me "how" I do what I do, how can I do so much stuff? I had to do some soul searching and really figure out what makes me, ME. What makes me tick? What motivates me to accomplish projects in my life? And of course, I'm a *"Why Girl."* I find when I know the why, it makes things better and easier for me. So, part two is about different qualities that make me tick and other short stories from my friends.

When I graduated from high school, my Mom always wanted me to be a nurse on the burn unit, she felt that since I had been through a burn injury that I would be a great nurse, but I just didn't feel like nursing was my chosen career. I was also very concerned about my hearing and since I couldn't hear high-pitched sounds, I felt I would make a bad nurse. I also wasn't sure that I wanted to deal with watching other burn survivors go through pain and putting them in pain in order to help them heal.

I did go to work at the hospital where I recovered from my burn injury, but as a health records clerk, not a nurse. While working in the Health Records department a  doctor asked my co-worker what my name was. She told him and he  recognized me as the two year old who got burnt in 1968. He called me over and told me he was one of the doctors who worked on me when I first got burnt. I could tell he was very happy to see the two year old from 1968 had survived against all odds, he had a giant smile on his face.

This happened again with a nurse who stopped me to tell me that the room I was in collecting the charts from was my room, and that she was one of the nurses who looked after me when I got burnt in 1968. She told me a few stories about how worried they were about me and how amazed they were that I lived. I didn't know what to say to her, let's just say it was very weird being in my room.

*Dear Kelly,*

*I've been inspired and, in some cases, personally mentored by some great speakers over the years. I'd like to share a few recollections and a few lessons from their inspiration.*

*I recall watching veteran entertainer Art Linkletter mesmerizing his audience, then waiting for Dr. Vincent Peale to go on at the Calgary Jubilee Auditorium. (Circa 1972) Off stage Dr. Peale sounded and acted like a typical grandpa; a typical 65 plus year old man, walking slowly on stage to thunderous applause, after being introduced by MC Don Hudson, CSP, CPAE. I wondered how he would do?*

*He was amazing! For nearly an hour he captivated that audience with the power of his 'enthusiasm' and the power of that gravelly, vibrant voice. Story after story unfolded about what we could do with our lives if we believed, really believed.*

*I was inspired... I believed... and a strange thought entered my mind..."I would love to be able to do what he was doing!" Well... many years later!*

*My advice to you and your readers:*

- *Show your passion - it moves people!*
- *Tell your own stories*
- *Take risks if you want results*
- *Use powerful words to explode the mental images of your stories*
- *Connect from the heart and share the little things. They matter!*

*Bob 'Idea Man' Hooey*
*www.ideaman.net*

# BECOMING AN ENTREPRENEUR

When I was 19, I met Max who moved in with me and we lived together for 10-years before we got married in Mexico. During our time together, we caught the entrepreneurial bug and tried a few different network marketing companies and other businesses. Our first business was a foil printing business.

Our first attempt at business proved to us how time consuming a foil stamping printing business is and how unprofitable it can be. We decided to sell the equipment and move on since the business proved to be neither of our passions. Good thing we both kept our jobs during that entrepreneurial episode.

At one time, we also decided that we wanted a balloon business. I saw in an entrepreneurial magazine that there was a talking balloon business opportunity. I sent away for the $30 starter package and we decided to pursue it. Again, another wacky idea, but it turned into something else that was more real.

During this opportunity, we realized that we both had a passion for decorating and entertaining with balloons. Max loved balloon entertaining and learned how to make balloon animals and entertain kids and adults. He quickly learned that he had a passion for it.

I realized that I loved the decorating part of balloons and wanted to become a designer. At one point, we both quit our jobs and moved to another province to pursue our balloon decorating and entertaining business there.

When we got settled in our new rental house I decided there had to be a way to market our decorating and entertaining services. We only knew two people in the whole town and that was his sister and brother-in-law. How were we going to market ourselves in a small town where we knew NOBODY and there was already one balloon store in town and we didn't want to set up a store?

I decided the two markets I wanted to attack were the wedding and corporate markets. To attract the corporate market I went to the local radio station and proposed a "Boss of the Week" promotion. All week people could nominate their boss and at the end of the week the radio station would pick a winner, announce it and within the hour, I would deliver a balloon basket and other prizes that we had collected as donations from other local businesses. This was also a great way to meet the business owners while promoting our business on the radio for free. The radio station loved the idea because it gave them a fresh new idea to promote and had businesses phoning them. I like free promotion!

The way I attacked the bridal market was by setting up a Bridal Club. I went and introduced myself to all the wedding-related businesses who would be interested in tapping into the bridal industry. I set up monthly breakfast meetings and we shared leads plus we also decided to organize a bridal fashion show. Again, another way to get the bridal-related businesses referring me to their brides without us spending a dime on advertising.

The bridal club members loved the club because it also got them referrals. I found a way to generate low cost marketing with high value direct to their targeted audience. Nobody in that town had ever taken on such a challenge before.

Eventually, Max and I decided that the town was too small and that we wanted to move back to our home city and be close to family again. His brother brought out a trailer, picked us up and brought us home. At that point, I went and got a job and Max went to work building our balloon decorating and entertaining business from home.

Eventually, our passion for balloons led to us taking over an old balloon store location that ceased operating. Our business exploded overnight. After a year of owning a retail store we decided to sell it to an employee of ours and move on to starting up a production company and eventually a bath tub reglazing business. During that time we also tried a couple different network marketing programs, but didn't find one that we were truly passionate about.

Twice I was also elected President of the Alberta Burn Rehabilitation Society. Great experience, but challenging. The first time I was only 21-years old. I enjoyed being President because it gave me an opportunity to work with other burn survivors, but hated the politics of trying to please everyone and I had some strong opinions and had to make some very difficult decisions. The second time I was President was just before Alexanna was born, again, great experience, but very challenging.

Over the years, I also realized that my scrapbooking hobby was my passion and was something I wanted to make into a business. I created a mobile scrapbook store with a one-tonne cube van (more about that story later on).

My friend Bill, wrote a story about becoming an entrepreneur. What I love about his story is that it resonates so much with me, he talks about needing passion, vision, dreams and how with a thought he was able to create a business. He also talks about listening to your inner Fearless voice and not letting your inner Fearful voice get in the way.

*Dear Kelly,*

*People sometimes ask me how I foresee some of the next "big things" in business. My answer is to listen, see and act - fearlessly.*

*When I say listen, I mean truly listen to what's going on in the world around you. The news, books, teachings - take in everything that enters your mind as you journey through life. Listen to the needs and wants of people – from your family and friends, to business associates and others that you encounter along the way.*

*If you are listening, you will often hear yourself asking "what if?" What if this existed? Or what if I could make this happen? Would this make people's life easier? Would it make businesses run better?*

*If the answer is yes, start dreaming. Often. Let your mind visualize what life would be like if the product or service you've envisioned did exist, or if something that already existed was made or done better. Visualize the impact it would have. Dream of the success you could realize for you, your family and others.*

*Do not limit your dreams. Let them unravel to the highest level of success. No limitations. No barriers. No obstacles standing in your way. Visualize yourself standing on top of the world watching your ideas in action. Capture the contagious excitement you and others feel as your dreams unfurl.*

*As you dream, encapsulate your vision. Mark it down. Revise it. Dream and revise some more. Before you know it, you have the makings of something that not only could happen, but should happen. And you have the power to make it happen. But only if you act!*

*Unfortunately this is where most people fail. They don't act on their dreams. Instead, they let fear overcome their vision. Fear of no money to do what they want. Fear of not enough knowledge. Fear of what others might think. In a nutshell, fear of failure.*

*I know this fear well. When I started my first business, we just had new twins and my wife had quit work to look after them. We had gone from two incomes and not many expenses, to one income and triple the expenses - almost overnight.*

*I had a new job selling surveying equipment which didn't pay much, and making a go of things was a constant struggle. Yet as I worked hard trying to get ahead in my job, I kept hearing from people about a new upstart technology which enabled long distances to be measured not with a tape measure, but instead with instruments which could send an electronic signal to reflective glass and magically have an accurate reading down to the hundredth of an inch.*

*I began to dream of a world where if such electronic readings could be transferred to a new-fangled thing called a personal computer, surveying would simply never be the same. Projects could be built faster, easier and for less money. New jobs would be created. All I kept seeing was seemingly never-ending advancements in the world of surveying.*

*But so what. How could I make these changes happen? With barely enough money to keep my family alive, no special knowledge of the complex technologies I was envisioning and no idea how to create or run a business, what could I do?*

*What I did was channel my fears into passion, and to surround myself with people I considered fearless. Each time I encountered a fearful thought, I envisioned the exact opposite taking place. I decided to always envision success instead of failure, telling myself that nothing could stop me if I simply went ahead and did what I wanted to do.*

*Before I knew it I began running into all sorts of people who wanted to help. It was almost magical how my passion, energy and lack of fear radiated and gave me what I needed in return. From money to start the business, to exceptionally gifted people capable of doing what I needed, within a year of first visualizing what I wanted all the pieces had fallen into place.*

*Five businesses later, each one advancing the world as we know it, I look back and see that the famous Nike slogan "just do it" rings true for all successful people. Keep listening, keep dreaming and fearlessly keep doing and your vision of how things could be, will turn into how things are.*

*Bill Walton*
*Visionary Entrepreneur and Expert Business Consultant*
*www.sundancemktg.com*
*wvwalton@sundancemktg.com*

# SUCCESS

## Do you feel you are successful?

Yes, in many ways I am successful but I still believe I have room for growth to become even more successful. I have happy kids and I get compliments all the time about how good they are. They make me very proud as I never thought I would be a good mom. We made a decision for me to stay home with the kids when Alexanna was first born and I have only ever worked part-time at the most. We struggled financially, but it was still more important for us to have me home with the kids instead of working at a full-time job with the kids in daycare.

In other ways, I feel I am successful because I have been with Max for 24-years and when I was in school, I never had boyfriends. It wasn't cool for guys to be with me because I was different and considered the "ugly girl." As much as I wanted a boyfriend, they didn't want me, so having a long-term marriage has been considered a success for me.

I also feel I am a success because I am not scared to try things. I'm not scared to phone and ask for help, and if I am, I find a way around it in order to talk myself into it. I have learned that there are others who are better at some things than me, and if so, then I will ask them to do it.

## What advice can you give to others who are struggling to become successful?

First of all, you have to define what success means to you. My definition of success is to first be happy, secondly to have the ability to do whatever I want, whenever I want, thirdly to be financially stable and have unlimited income and fourthly, to inspire others and be inspired.

Never ever give up when you know deep down in your heart that you should keep persevering. When your inner voices are telling you different things, find the right people who will help you go in the direction you want to go in, while keeping your inner voice in the right zone.

So many times I was told I was crazy to try some of the things I have done, and if I had listened to them every time, I would not have experienced and learned how to do the things I know. Not everything will be a success, but you have to know when to stop and when to keep persevering. When your heart tells you to keep going, then you need to listen, no matter what others tell you, including that inner fearful voice. Find the inner voice that supports you. Give the fearful inner voice a "kick in the butt" and let your fearless inner voice "take over."

There were times I wanted to quit my business, but I kept looking at what my end result and my future could be and comparing what my life would be like if I kept my job and didn't follow my passion.

When I felt I wanted to quit, I would take a little break. Sometimes the break would last for a day, a week or even longer. I would put everything on hold and just go do something different. I would go to a woman's group or a networking event and get a fresh look at things. I would meet new people and then call them up and meet for a chat. I would find people who I thought were successful and ask for their advice about how they became successful. I would find ways to get inspired.

One time, I called Dale Wishewan, the creator and owner of Booster Juice. I saw him on television talking about franchising, and how and why he did it. I called him up and told him I was looking for a mentor and someone who was willing to help me succeed. We went for lunch and he totally inspired me to keep doing what I was doing and assured me that I was on the right track.

What I enjoyed most about chatting with Dale was how successful he was so quickly. He started his first Booster Juice and then within four months of opening, he was approached by someone who wanted a franchise. In their first year, they sold 14 franchises. So many times I was told that I shouldn't franchise until I had been in business for several years, but he was my proof that I should move ahead with franchising.

You know what else was cool, Dale told me that he was looking for someone to mentor. He said he had just told one of his mentors that if someone called him asking for him to be a mentor, he would take them on. The next day, he got a call from ME. Here was little me looking for help from a multi-millionaire.

## The Unsung Heros - My Friends and Family

My family always saw me as being a stubborn and strong-headed kid. They saw me face a lot of challenges, but they always knew I would never give up. I always saw my sister's life as easy, but she was always proud of me and my success. She saw me as courageous and brave and not willing to let myself down. She has always supported me and my willingness to try new things.

My friends think I am a success and they love watching me succeed. They love seeing me do what I say I am going to do. They have begun to realize that if I say I'm going to do something, I do it. No matter how big or small it is. They realize that I can accomplish anything I say I'm going to accomplish. My friends are also learning not to try and stop me. I don't do anything I don't think I can do and they know that. My friends believe in me, probably more than I do in myself.

My kids knows that if I come up with an idea, no matter how big or small it is, I can achieve it. They know that no dream is "too big" to accomplish.

When I tell my kids that I am going to do something, they just assume that it is being done successfully. Like when I applied to be on the Dragons' Den TV show and pitched my business to the Dragons, my daughter just assumed that we got the money even though we didn't. There was no question in her mind that we didn't get it. She was totally shocked when finally months later I told her that I didn't get it. She told me that it was their loss and that they were going to regret their decision. (I wasn't allowed to tell anyone the results until the show aired on television)

A lot of my family thinks I have a lot of crazy ideas, and they see me try things, they may see me getting knocked down, but they always see me get back up and try again. And they always support me because they know I'm going to do whatever it takes to do the next thing.

## What are your thoughts on the word "failure"

What is failure? There is no such thing as failure, there are just experiences in life that you need to learn from. I hate the word failure because it is so negative. I hate even saying that I have failed because I haven't. I have succeeded in learning something new every time someone thinks I have failed.

No matter what I do, something good comes out of everything. It is all in how you look at things. I always try to see the good in a situation and a way to make it positive. I think the word "failure" should be wiped out of the dictionary. Failure is not an option in my life. When someone tries to squash my dreams, I tell them I don't want to hear it.

I do not even like the word "can't." One coach told me that I wasn't allowed to say, "*I can't do something.*" If I want it bad enough, I have to say *"How can I do it?"* This is what I think about, how can I do it? And if I can't do it, then I really didn't want to do it. If there is something I really want bad enough, I will always find a way to do it. So if someone tells me, *"You can't do that"* I say, *"How can I do that?"*

For example, people told me how crazy I was to even think about shipping my one-tonne mobile scrapbook store 2,000 miles across Canada. They kept trying to talk me out of it, giving me what they thought were better ideas than mine. They thought I was crazy to even consider the expense of shipping the cube van there.

Before I even told anyone what I was considering, I had planned just about everything, other than who I was going to use to ship the cube van. I had it totally planned in my head, and justified why it was the best thing to do if I wanted my business to succeed.

I wanted to expand my business and find more potential franchisees for my mobile scrapbook store and a friend of mine was organizing the biggest scrapbook event across Canada. Of course I had to be there and with the mobile scrapbook store so the women could totally get the experience of it.

I thought about the excitement the girls would feel when they were inside my cube van, and how it's the atmosphere that gets them excited about wanting to participate in my business and how they too can do it because after all, I'm just a stay-at-home Mom with a wacky, awesome business idea. The cube van absolutely has to be in Toronto if I want to sell franchises at the trade show. There was no other way to do this trade show. The cube van will be there or I won't go, simple as that.

I started phoning all different kinds of shipping companies. I had an amount in my head as to what would be the most I would pay to get it there. I was getting quotes for double and triple what I wanted to pay. I was starting to feel a little down and not happy about having to pay triple what I wanted, that was definitely out of my budget. I left the situation alone for a couple days and then decided to call back to a company that I still was waiting for a quote from. I was shocked when he told me he could do it for the price I wanted to pay. I booked him on the spot and asked for the quote in writing.

One time, I let one of my friends put a little doubt in my head and my fearful inner voice started to kick in and decided to take over. I was getting a little down, so I decided to chat with another friend who is more of a devil's advocate. She is part of the reason I started my business (remember how I am, if someone tells me I can't do something, I do it, right? She was one of those girls who told me I couldn't do it and we all know what motivates me, right?) Yep, every time I had an obstacle, I thought of her and heard her voice saying to me, *"You can't do this and you will be bankrupt."* She actually did tell me that, so it wasn't hard to visualize her saying it. I worked 12-hour days for months to prove her wrong. I could not stand the thought of her being right; she motivated me to persevere even when I did not want to.

We had talks about this and we now laugh about it, as she is now one of my biggest supporters. So, back to the story, my devil's advocate friend and I were chatting and I told her I still didn't know how I was going to get the cube van to Toronto, and that I was starting to feel guilty about having to spend all this money to get it there.

We started tossing around some ideas. She also proceeded to tell me about another scrapbooking/crafting show that was being held the following weekend in a neighboring city and how awesome would that be for me to go for two shows instead of one. Double the sales meant that I could justify the expense to ship the cube van for two shows not just one. I could also use that time in between to meet with potential franchisees, meet some more media, attend women's meetings, and so on. Now there was absolutely no question in my mind about what I needed to do. I needed to find a way to make it happen.

## Ask for Help

I have learned two things on my journey; one is to not be afraid to ask for help and the other is, when you ask for help you must also be willing to receive it. At one time, we were so financially strapped that our power was disconnected. I did not know where to go for help, so I asked the Universe for help to our financial problems and for ways to make more money.

Within a couple days, I got a very long email from a family member offering to help us financially. I asked and so therefore I must receive, and so I did. It was very hard to open up and tell my whole story, but I had to. I had to accept the help because I really had no other place to go. The other benefit was that it helped me to move forward with my business because the financial aspect was being looked after. It gave me a renewed energy, desire and passion to work a hundred times harder in my business.

I have also learned to focus on the positive. When I focused on the money problems we were having, I attracted more bills and more money problems. When I started focusing on making more money, then all of a sudden more ideas came on how to bring more income into the house.

Once I shifted my thinking, I was able to get more positive results. I know sometimes it is hard to shift from thinking about the bills piling up to making more income, but it works. It worked for me. My phone started ringing with more bookings, my email started getting busier and I had more income opportunities than when I was concentrating on our bills. Concentrate on making money, not making bills and you will get more money.

You have to learn how to ask for help and also how to allow yourself to receive help when offered. Try to remember that it might be easier for someone else to solve your problem than you. You will get other perspectives on a situation just by talking to someone else, which may lead to your "Aha!" moment.

## When do you give up?

Now?
When you lose your passion?
Never?
Or, you don't even start?

That's a question I ask myself every once in a while, when do you give up or do you? Since I'm one of those girls who has multiple projects on the go, I am often wondering what is the right thing to do.

I am a visionary - a starter - I love when I get new ideas and then I start a new project and watch it grow from being an itty bitty idea, to a giant idea, to being in progress to actual completion. And then I make a decision about whether I'm going to do it again, continue it or put it on the back burner for another time or move on to the next big idea that interests me.

I'm always so hesitant to give up on a project because you never know when it's going to sprout and then explode into that awesome masterpiece you want it to be. Too many people quit just before it explodes.

Multiple times I have started a project, put it aside only to have it resurrected. A lot of times this is the Universe's way of making it happen when the time is right.

When do you give up? I still don't know the magic answer to that question, but many times I was glad I didn't give up on a project. You just need to follow your heart and decide what the best thing for you to do is. Making that decision to continue on or quit is very difficult.

*Dear Kelly,*

*I was 19-years old packing and shipping boxes full of greasy oil field parts. Not what I thought I would be doing when the teachers asked us what we wanted to "be" when we grew up. I had barely escaped high school with my diploma. In most peoples' eyes I should have been grateful for the job. I was making $50,000 a year, but I still felt like a failure. I couldn't help but feel there was more out there. I saw people all around me having success.*

*How were they doing it? What did they have that I didn't? Why were they having fun and driving nice cars while I was stuck in this warehouse obeying demands from my boss and sweeping floors? I soon saw that all these people had something I didn't. A business. I had always wanted my own business growing up. I had lots of ideas. Whenever I would talk to my friends about it they would always be plans designed for the future. One day we will do this! Well, I was 19 and none of those ideas happened. I finally hit my limit. I was sick and tired of being sick and tired. I was determined to have my own business.*

*I didn't know the first thing about running a business. All I kept thinking to myself was if these other guys were doing it there MUST be someway a guy like me could too. I told my mom about what I wanted to do. My mom learned over the years what would happen if someone said I couldn't do something. One day she told me about an event she saw coming up in the paper. It was about how to create wealth and learn about business and investing.*

*Like me, so many people there wanted to fire their boss and work for themselves. I WASN'T THE ONLY ONE AND I WASN'T CRAZY! The event was informative and inspirational and sent me down a path I was unfamiliar with. They recommended that if you wanted to be successful you needed to read books by other successful people. I had never really read books but the concepts they were talking about were intriguing so I wrote down some of the recommended books and went to the library. I couldn't put the books down. Everything I was reading made so much sense; it resonated with me and was stoking my fire. It wasn't long after that I came up with the idea for my first company.*

*The business would cost roughly $10,000 to get off the ground. I wrote a business plan with the help of a local business development company. The company liked the idea so much they wanted to give me $10,000 for a stake in the company. I didn't know the first thing about whether or not this was a good idea. I took my business plan and the proposal from the investors to my Aunt's accountant. He liked everything he saw but recommended I don't give up any stake in the company. He wrote me a $10,000 cheque that day in his office.*

*I couldn't believe it, this was real! I was excited and terrified at the same time. Then I did something crazy. I fired my boss and quit my job, my family, friends, and boss were all in disbelief. Some of them were a little negative. In my mind, my job was getting in the way of me becoming successful. I was armed with an idea, my work ethic, some start-up capital and my dream. And it turns out that's all you really need.*

*I surrounded myself with other great people and learned a lot along my journey. I have since started two other successful businesses. I look back on my journey so far and I'm proud. I'm proud I never let anyone steal my dreams. I'm glad I had the courage to lay it on the line back then. I can't help but think about how my life would be now if I would have stayed in my comfort zone; the relationships I would have missed out on, the places I've traveled to and the lessons I've learned about the world and myself. It takes passion and guts to be an entrepreneur. It's not always an easy path, but the path can lead you to some amazing places.*

*Jeff Samis*
*Add "Jeff Samis" on Facebook*

# DREAMS

*"The best way to make your dreams come true is to wake up."* --- *Paul Valery, French Poet*

I believe we have dreams for a purpose. Dreams are messages to us. I believe we have two types of dreams. One type is when we are sleeping and are usually crazy with hidden meanings and the other are dreams we can control and are things we would love to achieve in our lives. They are a way of telling us what we want in our lives.

Some people believe that dreams are just that, dreams. Never to be found, never to be achieved. I don't agree. I am a firm believer that dreams are meant to be found, not tucked away in Dreamland.

Sometimes dreams hurt because they are so big, they don't seem achievable or real, but if you want them bad enough, you can definitely achieve them. If you can visualize it, you can achieve it and I truly believe that. Thoughts really do become things.

My latest dream is to own a dolphin swimming therapy resort for people with disabilities. I have absolutely no idea how to achieve this dream, but I do know that one day I will have it. I will somehow attract a dolphin therapy resort into my life. Not now though, a few things have to happen first before I will be ready to achieve that dream. But when the time is right, the opportunity will present itself and I will jump on it.

What I do know is that it's not about the "how" and I don't need to worry about the how because the Universe will provide me with my dream. The Universe knows how, I just have to ask.

# Where is "Someday" on the Calendar?

The question of the day is where is "Someday" on the calendar, and when is it going to come? You might be asking, what is this about? My friend Kelly Walton told me that she had a dream to do something big someday. This got me thinking, I don't know of a calendar that has "Someday" on it.

When the heck is "Someday"? I only know calendars that have Monday, Tuesday, Wednesday, Thursday, Friday, Saturday and Sunday. Nowhere is there a "Someday." So if you keep waiting for "Someday" to come, it will NEVER come because it's not on the calendar.

How long are you going to wait to accomplish your dreams? Are you going to wait for "Someday" or start accomplishing your dreams today? I know "Today" exists. If you start today, you will start achieving your dreams, but if you keep waiting for "Someday," you'll never achieve them. Even little baby steps is better than nothing.

I prefer to start things today. When I wanted to know if men in wheelchairs could have sex, I could have waited for "Someday" to come, but no way, I didn't want to wait for "Someday", I wanted to know TODAY if they could. I didn't want to wait, so I started figuring out a plan and within a month I was creating and producing my own documentary with the help of my co-producers. If I didn't start taking action today, I would still be waiting for "Someday."

So, my motto is - Start following your dreams today because "Someday" will never come. My best friend, Janeen, lives by the motto, "Don't Postpone Joy." She really does, in every way. It works and I love it.

Dear Kel,

I'm a great believer in "signs." And I literally almost ran into my "Don't Postpone Joy" sign at a red light. For years, I had been struggling with a marriage that I was very unhappy in. People around us thought we had a great relationship, but then, you only let people see what you want them to see, don't you?

I had been trying to making things work, pasting a smile on my face but knowing that I was simply prolonging the inevitable. This day, I was particularly troubled and felt like I was screaming inside. I knew I needed out that I needed to be happy. Distracted, I slammed on the brakes to avoid hitting the car in front of me at the red light. On its bumper was a technicolour sticker, profound as it was neon, which simply said, "Don't Postpone Joy." I sat there blinking at it in disbelief. There was my answer. It was the sign I needed. I was finally going to call it quits.

Since then, "Don't Postpone Joy" has become my life's motto and remains front and center in pursuing my dreams. Life is simply too short to be miserable, have regrets or look back wondering "What if?" I just do things that make me happy now.

I have a fabulous new man in my life, am surrounded by supportive friends and family and have pursued my dreams of being a screenwriter and beyond.

When the economy tanked and work seemed to have fallen off a cliff rather than decrease steadily over time, I went back to my philosophy of not postponing joy. Life threw me some lemons and I was determined to make lemonade--glorious, sweet, delicious lemonade.

I was a single mother this time, and instead of freaking out and panicking; I assessed the situation and decided I could take the leap, follow joy and pursue my dreams. I took the opportunity to write a screenplay that has since been picked up by a producer and is scheduled to start filming next year.

Soon after, I also created and wrote a television series that is in development today.

So, don't postpone joy. You never know what jewels await...

Cheers, Janeen Norman
http://www.fabulouscorp.com/

# HERO

A hero is someone who gives you strength and courage to persevere. He or she is someone you look up to and admire because of their strength or something they have accomplished. A hero is someone you say, wow, that person amazes me for whatever reason you choose.

I have a few heroes, my Dad and Bette Midler.

My Dad is my hero because he taught me how to be a fighter in life and to never give up, no matter what. He was a boxer in the Pan-Am Games and won a bronze medal. Many times my Dad listened to me on the phone and no matter what he still listened to me, even when he thought I had some crazy ideas. He always told me, *"Kel you have to stick up for yourself no matter what."*

My Dad was someone I wished I could have seen all the time. I really didn't understand how he could move so far away from his two daughters. As I got older, it bothered me more and more. Little did I know that my business trip to Toronto with my mobile scrapbook store would be the last 12-days that I spent with my Dad.

When I shipped my mobile scrapbook store across Canada, I justified it as a business trip until the following month and a half happened after I got back. My trip became much more personal than ever and I realized how important my Dad was to me.

The one regret I did have was when my Dad dropped my friend and I off at the airport. For a brief moment I thought I should have my friend take a picture of us together, but I didn't. My Dad gave me a kiss and his last words were, *"Luv you Tiger, have a safe trip home."*

A week and a half later, I showed up to work and then got a phone call that my Dad had a heart attack. I was completely shocked, he was totally fine when I left him just 10-days earlier. My sister and I flew down to Toronto and spent a week with our step-mom and Dad. It was so hard for us to see our Dad in the hospital bed and we encouraged him to keep fighting, just as he would tell us.

When he was finally able to be woken up, there we were – his wife, my sister and I, his three most important girls. I know he was quite surprised and shocked to see us all and I'm sure was also quite confused. At that point, he still didn't know what was going on and why he was in the hospital. It had to be very serious for his best girls to be around him.

After a while we were able to talk to him, but he wasn't able to talk to us because he had a breathing tube. His next gesture to me was a shaking fist and him pointing his finger at me. And I said, *"I know Dad, if you wanted me to stay, why didn't you just say so, you didn't have to go and have a heart attack to get me back."*

After five days of being by his side, sadly, my sister and I had to go home back to be with our families. My sister also missed her first mother's day with her six month old baby, but she wasn't sad about that because she knew she would have a lifetime of them coming. Our Dad was number one in our eyes at that point.

We went home only to end up back at the hospital two weeks later. Dad had taken a turn for the worst and was not going to make the night. Again, another trip to Toronto, but this trip we knew would be the final one; he waited for us to arrive before passing on.

When Max and I met my sister at the airport I was telling her how bad I felt that I didn't take a picture of Dad and I that day I left a month earlier. She told me that she hadn't seen Dad in a year and a half. I knew then that I was thankful that I had those last 12-days with him. Those 12-days would be cherished forever, and at that point, I knew that my trip was not for business purposes. The trip with my mobile scrapbook store a few weeks earlier was the Universe's way of getting me to spend some amazing quality time with my Dad, in his final days.

Bette Midler is my hero because she reminds me of me. Bette is a singer, actress, comedian, wife, mother, philanthropist and just an all-around amazing woman. No matter what she does and whether she succeeds or fails, she gets right back up and does it again. I call her my hero because she helped me to accept who I am.

I had a hard time accepting that I didn't want to be just one thing in my life. Why couldn't I be happy doing one job for 25-years? I need to do many things. It is ok to be me and it is ok to not identify myself as one thing. I have done a million things in my life and will do a million more!

When I read my friend Lee's story, I could feel who her heroes were even though she didn't come right out and say who they are, I think her heroes are her precious daughters.

*Dear Kelly,*

*In the front entrance, I lay on the floor wrapped in the fetal position. I am rocking myself back and forth sobbing uncontrollably and screaming out for someone to help me, to stop the pain, to end this existence. My five year old daughter is due home any minute and I am filled with extreme anxiety. My heart is beating so quickly that it feels like it is going to explode through my chest, I am sweating profusely and am now having troubles breathing. My daughter arrives home and it takes every ounce of energy in me to appear remotely normal, however the tears keep coming. Her beautiful blue eyes are filled with fear and panic, she doesn't know what to do. She embraces me and keeps saying "Mommy it's going to be okay, you're okay." I call my husband and he comes home early from work, yet again.*

*Anyone who has experienced depression and/or an anxiety attacks knows the feeling of such hopelessness, fear and panic. In 2004, I was admitted into a psychiatric ward for depression and anxiety disorder, believed to have stemmed from untreated post partum depression. The desperation I felt on October 31, 2004 led me to make three attempts on my life, the last attempt resulted in my sitting by the reservoir with a broken beer bottle; as I began to draw blood at my wrist, two little birds flew into the lifeless tree beside me. I could see my two precious little girls; my angels, and at that moment I decided I wanted to live.*

*I made a conscious decision to accept how ill I truly was and to surrender. At that point, I was able to move forward with tiny baby steps, taking a minute at a time, then an hour, slowly rebuilding my life that had seemingly been stripped away.*

*The past five years have been a journey into finding and reconnecting with my inner strength and beauty. Speaking openly about my depression and attempted suicides, at times brings a feeling of discomfort from the person I am speaking to, a reminder that mental illness is still a taboo subject. For the most part, people will open up about their own personal struggle (or someone they love) with mental illness, I listen with empathy and compassion, and am proud to say I have inspired others to choose life instead of death.*

*Overcoming what I did, proved to me that I have strong character traits: strength, courage, resilience and an un-wavering gratitude for life! Since that time, I have dedicated myself to personal development and growth, which has brought clarity to my life purpose of inspiring and empowering others. This has led me to fulfilling my dream of running my own company, which through commitment, dedication and passion is proving to be filled with abundance & prosperity.*

*By Lee Horbachewski,*
*http://simpleeserene.com*

# CHAMPION

## What is a champion?

A champion is someone who knows you very well and empowers you. Your champion is someone who you can go to and will give you the honest truth about what you need to do. You can tell them anything and they know how to motivate you to get the job done.

The difference between a hero and a champion is that a hero is someone you believe in and a champion is someone who believes in you.

I have a few champions including my Mom, my sister, my husband Max and a few other great friends. One is my best friend, Janeen. She knows me so well that she can tell when I'm genuinely frustrated or just having an adult temper tantrum and she lets me know it. And what I like about her is that she is honest with me.

One time I had this idea that I wanted to make bumper pads for the bath tub so that when babies slip and fall in the tub they don't hurt themselves. She was honest and said, *"Hon, that won't work, seriously, don't waste your time."* She's a marketing and media genius and so I trust her opinion.

She knows which projects are going to keep my attention span and keep me energized. She also knows when to tell me I'm being stupid or crazy. That is, stupid in a good way, of course. When I have an idea, I talk to her about it, and there has been many times when she would tell me, *"Kel, I don't think that's going to work."* She keeps me headed in the right direction and she's not scared to tell me whether I'm right or wrong.

Now, when I'm in alignment – she tells me that too. She tells me when I'm on the right path and that I shouldn't give up.

This is a true champion. They stand behind you and are not scared to tell you what they think. They empower you to be the very best you can be. They find things inside you that you didn't know you had.

One day, my other champion, Charmaine, and I were talking about things and she was telling me about a conversation she was having with another eWomen Network member and how excited she was about Kelly, this girl she met, and how inspiring she was. That her life story is so incredible, and on and on and on about how great this woman was and how she absolutely had to have her speak at her event. I stopped her and said, *"Who are you talking about?"* and she said, *"YOU!"* I just laughed and said, *"Oh my gosh, I'm not all that."* She said, *"Oh yes you are, all that and more!"* I just couldn't believe that someone saw me as such an amazing woman.

This is the cool thing about champions, they see things that you don't and they help to encourage you to either see those qualities or find new ones.

Charmaine and I met at a Roaring Women business mixer. When I go to a business mixer, I always go by myself because then I'm encouraged to meet new people. When I get there, I walk in, and scan the room for people I either don't know or for anyone who strikes my eye. And not strike my eye in a, whoever is the most beautiful person, but strike my eye in that I get the feeling that I NEED to know that person. I don't know what it is or why I do this, but I do.

This one day, I scanned the room and saw this blond lady wearing a teal jacket. I had an "aha" moment. She was the one I had to meet, and if I didn't meet her I'd be mad at myself. She was just one of those women that I had to know and when we did meet, we just clicked instantly. We had a million things to talk about with not enough time to fit it all in. I knew she would be one person that I would develop a long term relationship with and we have.

She has been very instrumental in getting me started in following my passion as a keynote speaker. She pointed out the value in my story and how it had to be told.

She saw qualities in me that I didn't know existed and she encouraged and inspired me to follow my passion for speaking. Whenever there is an event that Charmaine thinks would interest me, she makes sure that I know about it. She is genuinely enthusiastic about me becoming a successful keynote speaker and inspiring others with my story.

Charmaine is the root of so many things that have happened to me over the last year. She has given me more courage and confidence than I have ever had. She has shown me that I am capable of accomplishing whatever I want in my life and that people DO want to hear my story and that I should follow my passion for speaking and inspiring others.

Everyone needs a champion in their lives. Your champion is the person you go to when you're feeling insecure and you need that one person who will pick you up, dust you off, wind you up and make you go again. He or she's the one person who doesn't forget how awesome you are and knows how to make you feel great about yourself again. Find your CHAMPION! I love my champions, they're awesome too and they never let me forget my purpose in life. *Thank you Charmaine and Janeen, you are AWESOME too!*

Following are two letters from friends of mine from high school talking about their champions in life.

*Dear Kelly,*

*During the summer of grade 11, I had the good fortune to work with a young man at the water park. I was immediately drawn to him. He was not large in stature, yet he walked and carried himself with the confidence of someone three times his size. He had a personality that drew me to him. He was only four years older than me, but when you are only 17, a 21-year old has a life-time of experience in comparison.*

*I quickly became friends with Richard. He would arrive every morning for his shift wearing some kind of crazy hat and loud shorts. He drove unconventional vehicles with pride. He left long philosophical statements on his answering machine that left the caller too stunned to leave a message. He would engage in discussions that would visibly make people uncomfortable to see how they would react. He strove to make himself different from everyone in every way he could.*

*The one thing I realized in witnessing all this was, he didn't care what anyone thought of him. Being a 17-year old who was never popular at school, overweight since childhood and average-looking, I would never dare to do something so risky, to be so 'un-normal', to draw attention to myself.*

*I am sure Richard saw how unconfident I was. As our friendship continued, I came to realize that Richard was slowly exposing me to 'uncomfortable' situations to teach me that regardless of what others thought, I had to be me and be proud of "all of me." I always tell everyone that it took years for Richard to teach me self-confidence. Richard created the 'me' of today. The confident, assertive woman I have grown into, is a direct result of what he taught me. Love yourself for who you are.*

*Despite the fact that we now live in different provinces, Richard and I are still close friends today, some 27-years later and he is my Champion. Each time I find I need a positive influence, I make sure to call him.*

*Dawn Ofner*

*Dear Kelly,*

*It never occurred to me that I was different, I had all my limbs, everything on the outside was normal. I could understand, but not tolerate the whispers about those who looked different physically. I was not scarred and yet the bullying and silent scorn became an over-whelming part of my existence in high school.*

*You dear Kelly, were never a part of that crowd that mocked me, you saw in me an ally, another voice in the campaign to let those around us know that being different is OK!! No one had ever stood by me in such a way, so imagine my joy when 25-years later, three weeks before our 25-year high school reunion I received a message from you on Facebook!! The magic that social networking has, reunited me with you my friend, but most importantly you have reunited me with a family I thought I lost forever.*

*Alcoholism is a devastating condition, and I had succumbed to its power over me, and in the process walked away from everything in the world that meant anything. I even moved to another country and lost all contact with my family and they had no clue how to find me. As we chatted, I expressed the regret of not having kept in contact with my family. What should appear in my chat screen was the phone number that would change the course of my whole life. You gave me the phone numbers to my family and now I have my family and life back.*

*A champion is defined as "a person who fights for or defends any person or cause," and I must say Kelly you personify that definition. In your presence, all are made to feel worthy. Please continue the fight, there is so much further to go and I know you are the one to take us to the next level.*

*Michael McDonnell*

# MENTORS

Mentors are like coaches. A mentor offers support, guidance and assistance to help you work through your problems and challenges in your business and/or personal life.

I have many different mentors. My mentors have helped me to make different decisions or to understand problems and situations. Depending on what my situation is, I determine which mentor to go to. When I have situations I want to deal with in regards to my speaking career, I go to my mentors who are successful speakers. When I wanted to know more about how to franchise my mobile scrapbook store, I went to my mentors who were successful franchisees.

The key to a good mentor is to find one or more who have expertise in the areas you need help in. It wouldn't do me any good to ask my speaking mentor how to franchise my scrapbooking business; he/she wouldn't know. Just like my franchise mentor wouldn't have a clue about how to develop a great keynote message. Each mentor has their own unique role in your life.

Don't be shy about asking someone to be your mentor. True mentors love being asked, it makes them feel honoured and proud that you want to learn from them.

I will never forget how I met Jack Zufelt. Jack put on his Facebook status that he was tired of people just becoming his friend because they wanted to present him with a business opportunity. He wanted people to really "become his friend" first and get to know him then they should present him with their business opportunity.

I commented on Jack's status and said that I too was tired of people presenting me with their business deals and especially ones that didn't work and that if they really knew anything about me, they would know that I'm very focused on being a speaker and that I'm not interested in pursuing other crappy business deals at this time. Jack was very polite in his status, whereas I was very blunt and direct.

Anyways, Jack really liked my comment and directly emailed me about it and so of course we got chatting about what each other does and need help with. Jack loved my story about being a burn survivor and wanting to help others feel their beauty from within and offered to help me become a successful speaker. He became my mentor because he sincerely wants to help and I sincerely want help. *"Thank you Jack, I am very grateful for having you as a mentor."*

Coaches are also great, but I truly believe that you need to find a coach who can coach you in your specific areas you need help with, someone who can help you grow. One time I was approached by a group who wanted to help me market and grow my business. They spent two hours evaluating my business and then presented me with a marketing plan the following week. The marketing plan didn't give me any new information or offer me anything that I didn't already know. Not only that, but they wanted a gazillion dollars for something I was already doing. Needless to say, I didn't spend the gazillion dollars, I went with a different coach. I went with one who was specific to my industry, a speaking coach, Cheryl Cran.

What better person to coach me than someone who has done it? My speaking coach has been speaking for 15-years, she knows what works and what doesn't. It would make absolutely no sense for me to hire a coach who doesn't have experience in the speaking world. *"Thank you Cheryl, you have helped me to see what I need to do in order to succeed and have inspired me to take action."*

*Dear Kelly,*

*When I think of my spiritual mom I think of the word mentor. In Webster's dictionary the definition is, a person looked upon for wise advice and guidance.*

*Our journey began in 1990, I knew of this lady named Beryl for quite some time and felt an instant connection to her. I had been without my own mother for 35-years and as I watched this lovely lady, she mirrored an image of the woman I would love to become. She was full of joy and faith in God that was contagious when you were around her.*

*My life had been full of challenges and my faith had already been tested many times. My husband and I had just celebrated our twenty-fifth wedding anniversary and he had decided he wanted to end the marriage and start a new life with someone else.*

*I remember the day that Beryl and I met at the garden club meeting in the neighborhood. This particular day I just said a few words to Beryl; I needed to tell someone that my husband had just moved out. Divorce was something I had feared forever and now it was happening to me. Beryl folded me in her arms and said, "It will be all right." We went through many months of counseling to rebuild a very broken marriage.*

*On March 9, 1991 Rusty and I had a new marriage and were renewing our vows in our church, standing side by side. All our prayers had been answered until two years and five months later.*

*August 28,1993 we were in a near fatal motor home accident and Rusty and I were both badly burned. Once again Beryl had a full plate to pray for, times were sad, not knowing whether we would live or die. Rusty only had a 9% chance of living and we were not sure if I would ever walk again. It was a difficult time for all of us. I am sure it was hard to look at me and listen to me cry in such sorrow and pain. The recovery was long and hard. Many hours, days, and months went by, and Beryl was there to support and encourage me all along the way. I will be forever grateful for her love and care. She has been the best teacher and mentor I could ever have.*

*By Sue Lugli*
*www.susanlugli.com*

# VISION

## What is Vision and why is it important?

Every thing is an idea, started by a thought found in someone's head. Someone thinks, *"What if I had something like this to solve this problem?"* Or, *"I wonder, if there's other people like me who would want to do this?"* Or, *"If I made something like this, would other people buy it?"* Or, *"If I brought this person here, would people want to listen to them speak or hear their music?"* From their thought, a person creates their vision. A vision starts as a thought, with someone thinking they have the solution to an issue, and can create it.

And it's true; whatever you think about you can create. Your brain will help you create your vision.

Vision is extremely important to me. When I get an *"aha moment"* and think I would like to create something whether it be a book, a business, or an event, I have to be able to visualize it in my head first.

For example, when I was looking for a way to take my scrapbooking passion and make it my business, I was thinking about all kinds of ways to create something new and unique. I wanted to create a business that every scrapbooker would be excited about and want to access. I created a vision of a mobile scrapbook store. A cube van that traveled from event to event, full of scrapbook supplies that was a miniature store.

This mobile scrapbook store would provide a place where customers could come inside and pick out their favorite products, buy them and leave, rather than wait on an order from a catalogue. I wanted something that I wouldn't have to spend a tonne of money on overhead or staffing, with very minimal monthly costs. This business also had to be something I could schedule my own time around, as well as go to where my customers were and especially to small towns that didn't have any scrapbook stores.

I worked at a scrapbook store and realized that I would be committed to very high amounts of inventory and overhead costs. Not only that, but my time would be consumed by the store. The store would become number one in my life, not my family, and I didn't want that.

I also tried selling scrapbook supplies for three different catalogue shopping companies, very quickly got bored of their product lines, and realized that their catalogues limited me. I also hated having customers fill out orders that I would have to order from head office in the United States, then wait for their orders to come in, and then get back in touch with the customer again in order to give them their order.

What a long and time-consuming process, that I absolutely hated. I know there is tremendous value in getting together with your customers multiple times, but I just felt it to be more of a long drawn out process, especially because when scrapbookers see something they want, they want it now, not a month from now.

I didn't like being a catalogue shopping consultant. This realization had me thinking that I somehow wanted to find a way to combine the product selection of a store with being mobile. I wanted to bring a store to the customer where they could shop from me and take products home that night, plus have a bigger selection of products to choose from than just a catalogue. I wanted to be able to cure the *"I want it now"* syndrome from catalogue shopping.

One day, I had an "aha moment." I approached Max and said, *"What do you think about a mobile scrapbook store?"* He said, *"That is f___n brilliant, when are you starting?"* I said, *"What? You were supposed to say no to that crazy idea."* And he said, *"Nope, DO IT!"* And I did. I had no business model to follow, but I knew I could do it.

I started to plan the whole mobile scrapbook store. I found a cube van to purchase, put together a budget, arranged the financing and made it happen. I could visualize the inside of the cube van, the outside, the products on the hooks, customers going inside, getting excited and actually paying me money for supplies. I had a vision and it worked. I had the vision of being the 7-11 of scrapbooking on wheels.

Another example of vision is when Max and I owned our balloon decorating business. The only way to get education was to spend big bucks and travel to the United States. In those days, the Canadian dollar was worth almost half the American dollar and it was very expensive to travel, so I thought to myself, I wonder if there are other balloon artists like us who would like to have education brought here in Canada. I called all the balloon stores in Alberta and sure enough they wanted to be better educated so that they could sell more balloons and increase their sales.

The reason they weren't going to the balloon conventions was because of the same reasons we didn't want to go. The dollar was too low and travel was too expensive, but they were certainly willing to spend their money here in Canada. They wanted education and were willing to help organize a balloon convention here. I took on the challenge with a few other balloon store owners, and planned the first ever balloon decorating convention in Canada.

I approached the top balloon manufacturer in the world, in both Canada and the United States (the same company), plus the top Canadian distributor with my idea for top balloon decorating education to finally come to Canada. By training balloon artists, we'd become better skilled, which in turn would help the stores sell more balloons, which would lead to more balloon sales for the distributor and the manufacturer.

The American manufacturer was totally on board because I was also willing to let them do certification testing at our convention. The Canadian distributor was on board too, but the Canadian manufacturer didn't believe I could do it. The man I spoke to said, *"No way, it can't be done."* I said, *"Watch me."* I didn't let his opinion stop me because I had 20 balloon stores, the distributor, and the American head office backing me. I continued ahead without his support.

A month later the Canadian manufacturer phoned me and said, *"I hear you're still going ahead with your convention?"* And I said, *"Yep, you bet."* He said, *"I'm in, what do you need?"* I said, *"I need three things, your presence at the event, your database and balloons for classes and decor."* I had him for all the right reasons. I very easily could have quit when he told me it was impossible, but I thought there's no way one person is going to tell me I can't do it when I know I can.

We had 100-people at the first Canadian convention. This may not sound like a lot, but this was before the birth of the internet when traditional marketing methods had to be used and there was no such thing as email or viral marketing.

What was the vision in this situation? I had a vision that I could bring together balloon artists, manufacturers, suppliers, distributors and educators to create top education in Canada. I could visualize people going to the classes. I could visualize people teaching classes. I could visualize having a banquet and the room decorated with a thousand balloons like a Mardi Gras, and everyone dressed up with masks that they made in class. I could visualize each day of the whole event from start to finish. I knew how to organize it to make it flow, and what I didn't know, I asked for help. I also planned the event with zero dollars of upfront money.

The whole event was planned in my head before I did anything else. I just had to do one step at a time and everything would fall into place and happen. And sure enough, it did. This whole event could not have happened without my starting vision.

Many times people have approached me about doing events for them, but if I can't see their vision, I can't take it on. I can't get excited about the event without the vision. Vision is extremely important to me and if I don't have a vision in my head, I just can't make it happen. I'm not sure why, but that is just the way it is with me. When I have a vision, nothing can stop me. I run that vision through my head a million times, I see things flowing and with that vision, I'm able to see what works and what doesn't. Vision is what gives me my passion.

*Dear Kelly,*

### *Action + Faith = Living Your Dream*

*In our pop-culture world of models, celebrities and plastic surgery, I dreamt of finding a way to celebrate and acknowledge the day to day contributions of 'real' women. I wanted to see less of the females airbrushed to perfection and more of the women I knew and was working with every day.*

*I wanted to provide inspiration and validation to women who were making relationships work and raising a family; who were healing an illness or studying hard in school, volunteering and coaching and fundraising while building better communities and leading those around them; women who were building their own business or rocking a career; women who were committed to leaving the world better than they found it. I felt called.*

*I was working as an elementary school secretary when my Vision led me to become a magazine editor and publisher. Although I had a natural creative streak and some basic business experience, I lacked a degree in Journalism and had no publishing or design experience. The decision required an exhaustive learning curve and extensive risk, but the reward was Real Woman Magazine.*

*Many that I respected questioned my decision and attempted to discourage me. They felt they were saving me from rejection, failure and heartache, but I was love-struck by the dream and would not be discouraged. I ignored the warnings and persevered. Four years, over one hundred featured females, twenty two paper issues and one e-magazine later the goal of encouraging women to recognize and celebrate their own lives, stories and contributions has been realized.*

*Even though the finished product looks nothing like the original Vision, Real Woman Magazine continues to thrive, featuring inspirational women, ideas and philosophies. And the reality is far bigger and better than I could have ever dreamed it to be.*

*That's the magical thing about Vision. It comes from deep inside your soul. It is your connection to God and Spirit and the Universe. Following your Vision is how you become your best version of your Self. It's how you reach your highest potential. When you pay attention to the Vision - when you're brave enough to follow the dream, to nurture the calling, to take action and to be willing to be led by something bigger than yourself - you make your dreams come true.*

*By Kim Berube*
*www.realwomanontherun.com*

*Dear Kelly,*

*Have you ever had a moment in time where you became crystal clear on your purpose? My clarity came on a dusky evening drive home, as we turned off onto a west facing highway. There ahead of us was a breathtaking, beautiful and powerful sunset, different from any other I had seen in my travels, or here at home. It was as if it was speaking to me. What was the message? My thoughts turned to my husband who would be in Africa in a few months, volunteering at an Aids Mission. I was desperately trying to orchestrate a fundraiser to support the mission and families. Not even one ticket was sold yet and I was in fear of a great failure. Was there a message for me in this beauty and wonderment? I believed I could see a silhouette along the horizon, of children laying on dirt floors in grass, mud and tin huts, seeing the sunset out their doorway and crying. For many children in Canada, sunsets would bring joy and anticipation of a new day. But to millions of children in Africa, a sunset likely means more pain, no joy nor hope on the horizon. Children trying to fall asleep under the sunset, are pained with hunger and no hope of when they will have food again.*

*This sunset engraved the assurance that I was doing this fundraiser for the right reasons. The children, the community and the struggling Seed of Hope all needed support. For the next few Sundays my two minutes to promote my event in church was about that sunset and how different it would be seen by those children so far away.*

*By 7pm, Oct 26, 2006 I was in great awe of a church filled with 184 people, 70 homemade pies in the kitchen, great entertainers, and over bidding on auction items. From nearly cancelling the event 10 days prior, to raising $13,249.17 in one night was beyond my vision. The glow of that sunset continues to warm our hearts, fuel our desire to serve and inspire our gifts to humanity.*

*By Jo-Ann Grimwood*
*www.sendoutcards.com/josco*

## PASSION

*"Passion is a journey, not a destination. Every day choose in favor of your top passions, and you will soon find yourself living a passionate life"~ Janet Bray Attwood and Chris Attwood*

When I have a vision, an internal passion develops inside me. It is like an energy that fuels me and keeps me energized and interested in the project. I believe in passion and that without passion, nothing can be accomplished. Passion is what gets me excited, crazy and energized.

When I have passion, I can't sleep at night, and work 20-hours a day. There's nothing that can stop me. I somehow find a way to work so hard that I only stop when my body is so exhausted it just won't keep running and absolutely needs to sleep.

Passion, for me, is when the thoughts are so strong in my head, they don't allow me to focus on anything else. I don't know how many sleepless nights I've had when I find my passion in something. There are times when I get so mad because I can't turn off my head and tell it to just go to sleep, but I also love the feeling because I know I'm following my passion and in alignment.

## How do you find your passion?

I honestly didn't know what true passion was until this past year. I heard lots of people say, when you follow your passion, the money will come. I knew it was a feeling I got and I knew it was something that kept me going, but I didn't really know if I had it or not. Not until I met Janet Attwood and took her Passion Test.

Last year, I participated in a seminar with Janet Attwood. She is the founder of the Passion Test. For anyone who doesn't know what their passion is, I strongly recommend her book. You will find the process is so simple, yet so powerful, and when you have discovered the five top passions in your life and start pursuing them, everything will fall into place, and you will discover what you truly want to do in your life.

I will never forget meeting Janet. She has this warm and loving aura about her and when you see her, you can just see the compassion she has for people. She genuinely wants to be there and help you. She stayed after the event and gave everyone as much time as they wanted with her. If you needed 30-minutes of her time, then she gave it to you and everyone else waited. If you needed an hour, you got it. If you were in tears, she made sure when you left, you felt inspired about your life and had the strength to keep moving forward. When it was finally my turn, I'll never forget the feelings I had. She took both my arms and said, *"Kelly, your scars are your gift, use them, people want to hear your story, tell it."* This was when I decided that I would follow my passion and inspire others with my story and be a professional speaker.

You see, I never saw the value of my story, or how I could help others. I couldn't understand why people thought I was so inspirational. Yeah, I got burnt, so what! Lots of people are burnt, I am no different than anyone else. I am just me.

Like my best friend said, *"Kel, you have spent all your life trying to avoid the spotlight and now it's time to shine."* People want to hear my story because, for the most part, most people aren't like me. They don't know how to discover and pursue their passions.

A lot of people don't know what they want to do in their lives. I was just like that too at one time, but now, when I speak to others about my story, I get a feeling inside my body. It feels like a vibration, and when I leave a speaking event, I feel it. This is when I recognized that I am truly following my passion, I never had that feeling before with other businesses or jobs that I did.

Now that I know what that feels like, I will never do something that doesn't give me this feeling. I know now that I could never give up being a speaker, and I am looking forward to going wherever this passion takes me. I will hopefully inspire millions of people to find their true beauty from within and to take the risks in order to get the rewards they want.

I decided I wanted to do a documentary about people with disabilities and sexuality. I had always been curious about whether men in wheelchairs could have sex. Some people thought I was crazy that I wanted to know. Some people just automatically assumed that someone in a wheelchair could or couldn't without really knowing, but a lot of people had the same questions as I did, and were just as curious but didn't know how or who to ask.

I went to a business mixer and met a man who worked for a television production company that was looking for more projects to work on. I introduced myself and asked if we could get together so that Max and I could pitch him the idea. I said right up front, *"Have you ever wondered if men in wheelchairs could have sex?"* He gave me a weird look and said, *"Actually, yes I have, and come to think of it, can they?"* He was hooked and wanted to know more!

I told him that I wanted to do a documentary about people with disabilities and sexuality; I wanted to answer those questions that everyone is afraid to ask. He said *"Great, let me pitch it to my partner and I'll get back to you."* Within a week, we were producing a 30-minute documentary. This project brought a lot of challenges, especially since I had never produced a documentary before. I didn't have the foggiest idea about how to start, but fortunately, my new partners knew what I didn't know. My first two challenges were to raise the $20,000 to produce it, and then finding couples with one or both of them having disabilities, and who would want to expose their sex lives and share their intimacy with others.

One of the great things about when I have passion is that the Universe does truly provide me with what I need when I need it. For example, obviously I had to find people for our documentary. Fortunately, my new partner's girlfriend had connections with a professor at our local University who taught sexual health. When we told him my idea he jumped on board. Little did I know, sexual content for people with disabilities is extremely limited and outdated by at least 20-years. He had been searching high and low for content like ours. I was excited. I met a fabulous resource who was definitely onboard and had the same vision as I had. He had totally bought into the concept and was ready to give us whatever we needed to produce it. Not only did he have fabulous resources, but he also had money to pitch into the pot.

A stigma that I had to address was the "you're producing porn?" issue - Absolutely not. If they told me I was prod-ucing pornography, then I knew they didn't get the concept, and I had to explain it further. This documentary had nothing to do with pornography; it had everything to do with people besides myself wanting to know if people with disabilities still had the same sexual desires and capabilities as so-called "normal" people.

I didn't let people's thoughts deter me. I was on a mission, and I had a passion for producing this documentary so I wasn't going to let them stop me. The interesting thing is, once they saw it, they understood, and were very curious about the content. And in some cases, people even said they wished they had a disability so they could have the experiences some of the participants were talking about. In many cases, people with disabilities have a better sex life because they have to focus on their disability in order to achieve better intimacy. They have to find ways to communicate and satisfy their needs in other ways, it gives them permission to communicate better.

Many times we had people say they wanted to be in our documentary only to find out later that one of the partners wasn't truly comfortable about exposing their sex lives to others, and that was ok. I knew what my purpose, vision and passion was with this project. I knew I would be able to find enough people to finish it.

One of my most memorable moments with this project was finding Jamie. I had heard through the professor that we were working with that there was a male entertainer in our city who had a car accident and became a person with paraplegia, and may be perfect for our documentary. Can you imagine what was going through my head? A male dancer of course would have a huge ego about his body and body image, but then to have his whole world shook upside down by not being able to walk and get all that attention from women, confined to a wheelchair for the rest of his life? I absolutely had to find him. I asked the professor if he could find him, but nobody knew his name or where he was. He even phoned the Paraplegic Association and they didn't know his name either.

Well, this sent me on a mission; I knew there had to be a way to find this male entertainer. Our world was way too small, my passion for this project was way too big, and therefore I wasn't going to let anything stop me. So what did I do? I got the yellow pages and looked up male entertainers. I phoned all the male entertainment companies, knowing that someone would know the story and be able to find this man. I found him in three phone calls; and the next day I was talking to Jamie about his experience.

I had the passion to find Jamie, and I didn't want to let one person stop me from finding him. I knew Jamie would be a fabulous addition to our story, and we just had to have him. Sure enough, Jamie and his girlfriend were very willing to be a part of our documentary. Jamie wanted other people to know what he went through so that he could help others.

Jamie's story totally inspired me; especially his drive to never give up hope that he would walk some day. I felt pain in my heart. I couldn't imagine what it would be like to lose my legs, and not be able to walk, I just had scars, I could deal with that. But, even more devastatingly, to be a man who also lost the use of his penis.

*Dear Kelly,*

*I want to tell you about passion...as I have experienced it. Almost six years ago my husband took his life – leaving me devastated. It took me several years to get past the initial pain to realize that I wanted to live. I woke-up one morning and asked myself, what is this I am living? Is this life? So why do I feel dead inside? I did not die. My husband did. I am alive.*

*Okay, so if I am alive, why do I feel dead? If I am alive, I need to redefine being alive. I set forth looking inside my heart and soul to find my purpose in life. I decided to take some time off work to allow myself time to do this. The first thing I did was flew to Vegas. Why? I had no idea...it was something inside of me that said get on a plane and go to Vegas!*

*I did. I jumped out of bed at 2:38 am on a Friday night and booked my flight to Vegas on the following Monday. My daughter thought I had lost my mind. You have to realize I don't gamble, shop or drink! Vegas!? The entire time, I had no idea why I was going, I just knew in my soul I needed to be there.*

*I stayed for a week and while in the airport at Vegas, awaiting my departure flight, I went into the bookstore looking for something to read. I wandered through the store for about 20-minutes. As I went to leave the store, the cashier asked me if I hadn't found what I was looking for. I stated to the lady that I did not see anything that interested me. She pointed me into a direction and said "Go look over there."*

*The hair on the back of my neck stood up. I knew there was a reason for this. I was pissed off and in disbelief of this 'happening'; however, I followed my hunch to go look. I quickly ran through the books that were there and I already had all of them; however, I noticed a book called The Passion Test and I stopped. Immediately I knew this was EXACTLY the book I was looking for and the REASON I was in Vegas.*

*The rest is history! I couldn't put the book down. I got home and searched Google for the Passion Test. I booked into the first available session, took the Passion Test session and became a facilitator for Janet and Chris. My life has never been the same. I live from my heart, my soul and everything I set out to do from this center happens! It is being in the flow, following my passions – life is really this easy when one accepts the energy of life and follows their passions.*

*Sherri A. Scott*
*Conscious Connection Creator*
*createmylife@shaw.ca*
*http://create-my-life.com*

# PURPOSE

## What is purpose?

Purpose is when you have a reason for doing something, a reason for life.

When I have purpose, I feel focused. I feel like I am on a mission, that I have a reason for living and the Universe provides me with what I need to accomplish my goals. For example, when I was planning our 25-year school reunion, I was running into grads everywhere; on Facebook, at funerals, swimming pools, and airports. Everywhere I went, I ran into a grad. People even nicknamed me the "Grad Magnet." I had business cards printed up so that I could easily pass on the information for our celebration to them. I had a purpose: I had to find as many grads as I could. I helped to find 90% of the grads for our celebration.

Purpose in life is not just about being a good mom or a good wife; it's deeper than that. It's about YOU and what you NEED to do in your life to make you happy and feel fulfilled. If I do not have a purpose for doing something, I can't do it. When I lose my purpose, I feel like I've lost my internal world, therefore I'm lost. I have no energy and find it is very hard for me to get motivated. When I lose my purpose, I am bored and uninterested.

I constantly have to start new projects to keep my interests. I'm a great project starter. I am great at developing a vision, starting a project, getting it done and then passing it on to someone else who can continue it and keep it going. Then I move on to my next exciting thing, my new purpose.

My Popa taught me that I had a purpose in life. He knew when I got burnt that I wouldn't die; there was a reason that I got burnt. It was as though I needed to be burnt so that I could meet challenges, accomplish my life goals, and fulfill my purpose, whatever that was. There was no way a two year old burnt in 1968 should live through being burnt to 75% of her body; there had to be some reason why. My Popa always encouraged me to pursue my dreams, because I had a reason to live.

My purpose right now is to inspire people and provide my family with a great life. Many people have told me that I have made a difference in their life and inspired them. One of my dearest friends told me how being with me has helped her to feel more beautiful and accepting of herself. I helped her to feel like she is OK the way she is and that she really is good enough. I never knew I had that kind of impact. My purpose now is to inspire others by explaining some of the qualities and experiences that have kept me going over the years, and helped me to overcome some of my challenges.

**MY words of wisdom:** don't be afraid if your purpose changes. I know my purpose in life has changed many times over. At one time I felt my purpose was to look after my Popa. Max and I lived with my grandparents at the time. My Popa was my biggest mentor and hero in my life, along with my Dad. There was nothing I wouldn't do for my Popa and nothing he wouldn't do for me. He made me laugh and covered for me when I was a kid so that my step-dad wouldn't be mad at me when I did something stupid.

When I was 18, I went through a phase where I had to know why I survived. My Popa knew I had a purpose in life, but I didn't know what it was and I wanted to. Why would a two year old live through such extensive burns? Why did I come back to life after dying in my hospital bed? Why did I have to live through all the challenges and struggles of being stared at and teased and whispered about? Would I find a man to love and marry? Why did I have to be scarred and ugly?

I decided to get hypnotized to search for some answers. I phoned a bunch of different hypnotists and told them what I wanted to know. I wanted to go back to the day I got burnt. I wanted to know what really happened. I also wanted to go back to the day I died in the hospital and find out why I came back to life. When I was hypnotized, I determined that I had two purposes, my sister and my Popa. For some reason, they were my purpose and later in life, I would discover why.

My Popa still had his first brand new truck, a Datsun from 1966. This truck was the tiniest truck around, and when it was time for my sister and I to learn how to drive, my Mom taught us using this truck in the grain fields. This truck was a standard, and we found it very difficult to shift and learn on, but we didn't give up. We were very proud and honored that our parents thought we were ready to learn how to drive. I think I was only 11 or 12 at the time, but I had already been driving a lawn tractor for a few years.

When we were kids, we got to spend a lot of time with our grandparents. We had a house on the same acreage as them. This was the same acreage where I got burnt.

One day I was backing out of the Quonset shop with my Popa's little Datsun truck, but I had forgotten to close the driver's door. I kept backing up, forgetting I had the door open, and next thing you know the door is bent back. I went running to my Popa and he gave me a look and said, "Don't worry, we'll fix the door." I had no clue how he could fix the door, I was positive it was impossible to do. I was quite surprised as I watched my Popa bend the door back and no evidence was left that I had actually bent it back in the first place. I felt so bad, I'm sure any other adult would have yelled and screamed at me, but not him. He gave me the look that said everything, and he didn't need to say anything more as he fixed the door with ease. I don't think he even told anyone else what happened. This lesson taught me that my Popa could fix anything, even things I thought was impossible.

Then there was the time I told my Popa that we should build a kitty condo for the three kittens we had just adopted. Someone had left three kittens at the end of our driveway when I came home from school one day. I carried these three kittens to my Nana's house and asked if we could keep them. I knew my Mom would say no, so I asked my Nana first. My Nana didn't know what to say, but my Mom let us keep them. Surprise, surprise, maybe we did need the kittens to help get rid of the mice on the acreage.

I decided they needed a home, so I asked Popa if we could build a kitty condo and of course he said yes. We headed to the garage, but knowing that it couldn't be something small, my Popa and I built a three tiered condo with holes inside going from one level to the next, with carpet for the kittens to scratch. My Popa and I spent two days working together on this kitty condo.

These are only some of the fond memories of my Popa and I doing things together. He was also the one who taught me how to sew clothes, make perogies, quilt, and cut with right-handed scissors using my left hand. Anything I wanted to learn he taught me.

When my Popa was getting sick, I realized why he was the purpose for my life. We really didn't know how sick he was, until it was time to take him to the hospital. I still remember my Nana getting mad at him and I because she wanted him to change into a clean t-shirt before he left for the hospital. My Popa couldn't breathe and all I wanted to do was rush him to the hospital. I didn't care whether he had a clean or dirty t-shirt. I waited for him to change this time, but less than a month later, I didn't wait.

The next time we were heading to emergency, she wanted to go put lipstick on before we left. I was livid! I told her that Max would bring her to the hospital while I took Popa. She was fuming with me, but I wasn't going to let her stop me from saving my Popa's life. He needed to go to the hospital now, not half an hour later when she was ready.

I don't think she truly understood what it was like for someone to not be able to breathe. I visited my Popa in the hospital every day, and because of some of the drugs he was on, he had some wickedly funny stories to tell. One day he told me that he saw Max and I on television. He said they called us by different names, but he knew who they were talking about. He kept trying to remember what they called us and then he had an "aha moment" – they called us Mixx and Koki. When we decided to do our documentary about people with disabilities and sexuality, we called our production company Mixx and Koki Productions because we thought it was a cool name, and it had sentimental meaning.

I absolutely had no idea that he would die so quickly. I really didn't think he was that close to death. I still needed him; I still had more to learn; I still needed more time to show him how much I appreciated him and his wisdom. When he died, I lost focus of my purpose. I was devastated. It felt as though I had no other reason to live, and that my purpose was gone. Eventually, I found a new purpose and I was re-energized and able to focus again, but my Popa will always remain rooted in my heart.

One of my friends and business associates, Dianna Bowes wrote an amazing story about a different kind of purpose. She wrote about how certain people have had a purpose in her life and I found her story very inspirational and want to share it with you.

> *Dear Kelly,*
> *I have been in three major relationships, two men of which I choose to marry. The first man, was Larry, the love of my life, my high school sweetheart, my hero, my future. Never in my life could I imagine living without him in my life. And as much as marriage scared me, I choose to commit to him forever. Well, forever was 10-days short of one year of marriage. Larry, this beautiful young man, was taken from us after an explosion that injured other family members as well. The other two men were seriously burnt as well as other injuries, which scarred their bodies, as well as their hearts, with the loss of Larry. This family tragedy brought the family together and my respect for these other men and their families will always remain with me.*

*I was 21 and single, I had never really dated, and was terrified to be alone, but had to recreate my life. This was the most difficult time in my life, but it was also the best. I discovered a vault of strength, buried deep in this young women's body. People around me were confused by my resolve to move forward in my life, they were surprised by my ability to stand strong and not fall down and to be honest so was I.*

*Shortly after Larry's death, I met Doug, handsome, charming, fun, and in pursuit, he was not going to give up easily. We were both on the rebound, totally tuned out that we were very different people. But regardless, we married, and we both picked up where our other marriages left off. We did the picket fence really well, lots of friends, a busy family life. But we can only pretend for so long, and Doug could not keep up the act. I lost Doug in another way, through addictions, almost as bad, because I could do nothing to stop it, either.*

*After my breakup with Doug, I dated and met many nice men. I listened, I learned, I began to rediscover myself and what I wanted. Mostly I spent a lot of time and money on myself, learning who I was and what I wanted. I treated myself how I wanted to be treated, with love, acceptance and most of all kindness.*

*And just when I was feeling really great, being on my own, I met John. Nothing like the other two men in my life, Quiet, strong, and about as direct as any person I have ever met. He taught me about abundance, strength, business, and has allowed me to embrace my entrepreneur spirit. He supports me in every thing I do, and encourages me to go for it, whenever I say the magic words "I have an idea."*

*This could be a victim story, I suppose, but I think of all of these happening as a blessing. I decided early in the game, I had a choice to be bitter or better and I guess you know which way I went.*

*You may ask, what have I received from each of these relationships. With Larry, my first in many ways, he gave me his family, who to this day I still see and share my life with. With Doug, I was blessed with two amazing children, that is another story. And with John, I received my life partner, my teacher, my best friend. He pushes me when I need it and supports me when I need it more. I have never felt able to be myself, more than right now in my life. There is a poem that is titled, A Reason, A Season, or a Lifetime, it is my theme song.*

*By Dianna Bowes*
*Mother, Friend, Partner, Graphic Designer*
*Founder of the Fabulous at 50 Experience & Martini Party and Be Fabulous!! Magazine.*
*www.fabulousat50.com*

# PERSEVERANCE

What is perseverance? What does it mean? I looked the word up on the internet and the definition truly reminds me of myself. Perseverance is defined as: *determined continuation with something: steady and continued action or belief, usually over a long period of time and especially despite difficulties or setbacks.*

I think back over the years, about all the challenges I've faced and how, even though I was challenged, I still persevered and achieved many of my intentions. There are still a lot of things I haven't accomplished, but for the most part, I have done a lot in my life. I remember talking to a mentor who told me to think of a challenge and say, *"It's not I can't, it's how can I?"* Whenever I think I can't do something, I turn it around and say, if I want this really bad, how can I do this?

Occasionally I ask myself how I am going to overcome the potential road blocks ahead. I think out the whole plan, but then focus on the purpose and the outcome I want to achieve. I find if I focus on what I can't do, then I can't do it, but when I focus on what I can do, it all comes together. I truly believe that the Universe will provide the solution to me when the time is right, but not until I prove to the Universe and myself that I want it really bad and don't want to give in.

Some times, when I get frustrated because I can't make some-thing happen, I realize I just need to take a break and not think about it at all. I will ask the Universe for a solution and eventually it comes to me. When the solution comes, I pick up the pieces and run with it again. I have learned over the years that I don't have to make things happen instantly. At one point, my goal was to be working at full capacity, using all my potential and not be able to do anything more. I wanted all my time completely booked and my brain working at top potential, doing multiple projects all while working full-time.

At the time, it seemed ok to be pushing myself to that limit, but then I realized after a couple years that I was just spinning my wheels, getting sick, burning out and not accomplishing much of anything. I was letting people down because I couldn't get everything done. I was starting all kinds of projects, but only finishing the ones that truly had my passion and vision. I realize now, that it's ok to take more time to complete projects, do things well, and not focus so much on quantity but quality. I also realized that quality of life is more important to me and that it's not fair to me or to others to take on challenges or projects that truly do not interest me. Now, I decide if the project truly fits into my passion and vision and whether I can finish it or not. If there is any doubt that I cannot finish it, then I don't even take it on.

My best friend asked me to sit on a parent committee. I kept saying how important the committee was, and how it would be good to be on a school committee, but every time there was a meeting, I couldn't get off my butt to go. I kept asking myself, why do I always find excuses not to go? Why do I commit and then not follow through with this? And then I realized I didn't have enough passion or vision for this committee. It didn't give me enough self-satisfaction to be involved, so I dropped out before I even started going. I realized if I couldn't go to the meetings, I certainly couldn't do any work for them, and it's not worth being just a body attending a meeting with no passion.

I also have to remind myself that I don't always have to know "how" to do something; I just have to accept that somehow the solution will come. The Universe always provides what you need when you need it.

# How do I persevere?

I persevere by trying to find the little things that bring me satisfaction instead of always trying to find something big to keep me going. One time, I was getting really frustrated with my business and thought that nobody wanted my services, but then I got two emails within the hour for bookings, and then I was like, yeah, that's what I want. I guess people do want me, I just can't expect people to give me constant encouragement.

That same day I decided to count my blessings, I wrote down every little good thing that happened to me that day and I had 23 blessings and only two things that were crappy. Once I counted all the little blessings I had, I realized I needed to be grateful for what I had. That is definitely the challenge in being an entrepreneur; it can be very lonely at times. I totally understand when people call it being a solopreneur.

Some times when I get into a slump, I find a business mixer to go to and find a way to meet new people. I find it always helps me to meet new people and become inspired by them. Meeting new people always seems to give me a new energy to keep on moving forward and helps me find new ideas that I never thought of before.

Sometimes it is the negative nay-sayers that inspire me to keep at something. When I was building my mobile scrapbook store, my friend and I had an argument and said some hurtful things to each other. One comment she made was that if I didn't smarten up, I was going to end up bankrupt before I even started. Well, that sure fueled me up. Whenever I needed energy or something to inspire me to overcome more challenges when creating my mobile scrapbook store, I visualized her saying *"You're going to go bankrupt"* and then I would get mad and say, *"No f'n way am I going to let you be right about this, I will not go bankrupt, I will make this happen!"* and sure enough I found a way to persevere through my challenge. For some reason, she brought out my competitive nature and there was no way she could stop me. I found a way to create my mobile scrapbook store and generate customers who would buy from me, despite her nay-say attitude.

After a while we worked things out and talked about what happened. It was great to rekindle our awesome friendship. We both apologized, and she ended up having a new faith in me because I had created something from just a thought. She was amazed that I had absolutely no business model to follow; that I had found a way to make a 1500-square foot store into a 14-foot cube van. I thanked her for being my inspiration and driving force to getting me to achieve my mission.

I have always found music to be a big inspiration for me, helping me to persevere in life. One song that I feel explains how I feel is, 'The Climb' by Miley Cyrus. There are times when I feel like I am just climbing mountains and for what? There are times those mountains just felt way too high. It has taken me a few years, but I realize that it's just me, I thrive on the climb. I will never be happy working at the same job for 25-years like my Nana T did. I am the kind of girl who has done a million things and will do a million more. I have come to accept this about myself. I am just one of those girls who loves challenges and variety. I love to come up with new things to do. I am glad that I have come to accept that about myself.

I do not like the thought of doing the same thing for 25-years. I think I would get completely bored and lose my spirit. I struggled to understand why I did not want to be that way. How could I have security if I did not have the same job for 25-years? I had to realize that there is no way I would be satisfied; I absolutely have to have variety in my life. I accepted that this is just me, full of lots of little challenges and many accomplished projects; many mountains to climb, and that is why the song 'The Climb' fits me so well. I will always find another mountain to climb. I am actually very excited about where my future will take me. I cannot wait to see where I will end up and what other new challenges I may face. I know the Universe has lots in store for me and I can't wait to see it.

Another song that always seems to play whenever I find a road block is 'Tubthumping' by Chumbawamba. When this song first came out, I thought it was so crazy and then I heard the lyrics and the part that I loved and suited me best was:

*"I get knocked down, but I get up again*
*You're never gonna keep me down*

Over and over and over it says those two lines – actually 11 times at one point, and it was such a reinforcement for me that hey – you got knocked down so what, now get back up and get at it! I always found it so unusual that that song would play whenever I was in the middle of a challenge or at a brick wall. The song was a reminder to get back up – nothing is going to keep you down, you can do it!

For example, one time, Max and I were riding our pedal bikes from town to the big city. It would be an incredible accomplishment for me, as I am the least athletic person on the planet. It would also take an hour to get there, and there were some big hills to pedal up. We got to the half-way point and that was where my Nana and Popa's farm was (the same farm that I got burnt at). I told Max that I couldn't go all the way and that I was just going to stop at the farm and get the truck and would meet him in the city.

Max knew how to push my buttons, and so he told me I couldn't do it. He said that he knew I couldn't do it. Well that was it – there was no way I was going to let him tell me that I couldn't ride my bike all the way there. All of a sudden perseverance kicked in, and I kept going. I wasn't going to let him be right, and more than that, I had to prove him wrong. I could do it! And I did. I kept going until I got there, and then to my surprise, when I reached our ending point, I wanted to keep going.

It felt great knowing that all I needed to keep going was a little push from Max saying I couldn't do it. This was when I realized what would make me persevere; the down side is that he now knows he can push that button to keep me motivated in ways I don't want to be. grrrrr

Sometimes, in order to persevere, you need to take a break and then go back with a fresh mind and attitude. There were many times when I started my mobile scrapbook store, I got frustrated and then had to take a break. Or, like when I was trying to raise money for my documentary. Sometimes challenges would be put forth and I would have to raise more money to produce it, or a guest for the show would initially agree to be interviewed and then change their mind and I would have to find someone else. I believed in the project so much, that I had to accept that it couldn't be produced on my impatient road map. It had to be done on the Universe's road map. Certain things had to fall into place first before it could happen, it had to happen in sequence.

For me, when I had a problem that needed to be solved and I didn't know the answer, I would stop, ask the Universe for help and then eventually I would get an "aha moment." After this "aha moment", I could get right back at it with a brand new sense of energy.

Over time, I had to come to realize that life happens on its own schedule. Not only is there the Law of Attraction, but there is also the Law of Time, and the Law of Time states that everything happens in it's proper timeline and when the time is right. You must give the Universe time to put all the little details in place before you can have your dream.

I met a girl who told me she was interested in purchasing my mobile scrapbook store. She wanted it for the same reasons I started it. She wanted a business where she could stay home with her kids plus make an income. Eventually she told me that she was suffering from Post Partum Depression. I never would have known this because I didn't think she was depressed. I asked her to tell me about it, and these are her words about how she persevered through it.

Dear Kelly,

A year ago I was blessed with a beautiful baby boy. He was absolutely perfect. He loved me and I know I loved him but couldn't. He was this tiny little stranger I looked so forward to meeting and when I did, wanted nothing to do with him. I knew I was in trouble. I felt the shame, the guilt of it all.

At six weeks post partum, I was diagnosed with Post Partum Depression. A disease a lot of mothers face but are either too ashamed to go for help, or think it's their hormones. I wanted the help, but I was stuck in a rut. I felt alone. I felt embarrassed that I had PPD. Who wants PPD? No one. I kept it from all of my best friends. My doctor and I worked on a medical regime and it was working, but I kept getting stuck in this rut. My counsellor even helped. All three of us worked together. But it wasn't until my baby boy's father walked out when I truly realized the devastation this disease had caused.

I morphed into this person who didn't even know herself. It was a hard realization to accept, I was partly at fault but not. PPD happens even to the most "with-it" women. I moped around for a couple weeks feeling for sorry for myself. Then one day, it was like I got kicked in the pants and my whole world changed. I realized I had two beautiful sons who I had taken for granted before; and now I wanted to be the best mother I could be for them. I had a bright and promising future at my fingers tips; I had dreams that I had long forgotten that I wanted to achieve.

*I found the STRENGTH to pick up the pieces that were on the ground and the COURAGE to move ahead without knowing what laid ahead and the HOPE that my dreams would come true if I strived towards them and that my future is as bright as freshly fallen snow. I had a new zest for life. I discovered that no matter what storms I faced or bumps in the road I came upon, that a little rain and a little off-roading would eventually take me to where I wanted to be. Nothing is ever as bad as it seems, as long as you keep believing in yourself and "Keep Moving Forward." Only greatness lies ahead.*

By Kelly Walton
rootsandwingsimagery@gmail.com

If you have a passion, a dream and a vision you can never give up, you must persevere. You need to remember that no matter how bad or dark a day may seem you have to find a way to keep going. Maybe you have to take a break and do something different, but eventually you have to keep pursuing your dreams. You have to find your inspiration; listen to a song that you totally love to get you fired up again, get out of the house and go to a business mixer and meet new people, whatever it is that makes you climb.

The song moving me right now is called "Smile" by Uncle Kracker. Whenever I hear this song, I have to sing and get up and dance. I just can't stop myself, as this song motivates me and gets me energized. Plug into your inspiration, and get moving.

Some day try this experiment, listen to five sad songs and see how you feel at the end of the songs, then listen to five high energy songs and record how you feel. I noticed that when I listen to sad songs, I start to feel sad. My whole body chemistry changes and all of a sudden all I can think about are all the disappointments going on in my life. When I listen to high energy songs I somehow have more energy, desire and passion for my life. I can instantly shift my mood and attitude just by listening to different songs.

# POSSIBILITIES

I have always been able to see the world as full of possibilities; a world that could change at any time. I see the world as a place that could make me as happy or as miserable as I want to be. Many people don't understand how I can take a situation and see the good in it, and they don't understand how I can see a change as being a good thing.

A lot of people take a situation and instantly see the bad or negative in a situation. I take the situation, think about it and then see all the angles, opportunities or possibilities. Then I let the Universe take over. I believe everything happens for a reason, and that sometimes when we don't get what we want, it is because something better is coming along.

For example, our mortgage company was an American company; one of the many effected by the market crash. When we got our mortgage four years earlier we had no clue what the future would hold, and we certainly had not thought we would be affected by an American mortgage crisis since we lived in Canada. It wasn't until we got the letter from our mortgage company saying they weren't going to renew our mortgage that we realized we were in trouble. We were shocked! We made all our payments, so what the heck was going on? Even better was the fact that we didn't receive the letter until December 3rd, and they wanted us to have a mortgage in place by December 1st (two days earlier), and they sent the letter from their office on November 17th. Now how is anyone supposed to get a mortgage in place yesterday?

We phoned the mortgage company and asked what was going on and they told us they were going bankrupt and liquidating all mortgages, and that we had three months to get a new mortgage. This breathing room was the good news, the bad news was that Max was laid off from his job and would have to become self-employed again. I was a stay-at-home Mom at the time, also self-employed. This meant that neither of us would be good candidates for a new mortgage. Our mortgage broker eventually found us a mortgage at 7.23%. This rate meant our rate was going up not down, and that our mortgage payment was also going up. We were grateful to have a mortgage, but devastated that we were forced into this higher rate.

If all of this wasn't bad enough, we also couldn't get the deal done on-time and needed an extension. The mortgage company told us to sell the house or go into receivership. Neither option was a good one, as Max was at the end of his rope, but I figured there had to be something better coming. Somehow the Universe was going to look after us in some way; not sure how, but it would happen.

Our mortgage broker said the only way we can do this is if we have a co-signor. I kind of figured it would come to that and as much as it made me feel awkward. I knew what I had to do. There was no other option. If I was going to provide a house for my kids, I was going to have to swallow my pride and ask for help. Our mortgage broker had tried everything she could to get us a good mortgage, but she needed a co-signor to seal the deal.

So, I swallowed my pride and phoned my sister and told her the situation. It hurt. It hurt real bad that I had to go to my younger sister for help. I should be able to do things on my own, I shouldn't need help at this age of my life, but I did. My kids needed me to provide them with a home. And if we didn't have a mortgage then we would have had to rent and rent is actually more expensive in some cases than a mortgage. We would have been going backwards, not forwards.

Long story short, my sister and brother-in-law helped us and we were able to get a mortgage at 2.65% instead of over 7% and our payment went DOWN, not up. We were ecstatic!

I knew the Universe would take over and look after us. I knew that somehow the mortgage company going bankrupt was going to work in our favor and be a good thing. I knew there was a possibility that this would be good, not bad.

In the beginning when we got the mortgage company's letter, did we think it was possible that we could get a better mortgage than what we had? At first, no. We just saw how we had a major situation to deal with. We had three kids who needed a home. We couldn't lose our house no matter what; we had to find a way. Then when we kept getting rejection after rejection, it was looking pretty doom and gloom for us, but I believed in the possibility that ultimately we would get a mortgage, somehow. And all those rejections were great because we exhausted every possibility until we got the right mortgage for us and now we're in better shape than ever. I am forever grateful for the help my sister and brother-in-law gave us, and for my faith in the Universe.

Another example of possibilities is when I saw a competition on Facebook for the Every Woman Competition by Fashion Has No Borders. Do you really think there's a possibility that a burn survivor can win a model search competition? I wasn't really sure if I could or not, but I thought, hey why not give it a chance and see what I can do? Maybe there is a possibility that I can get accepted; someone might like me and my story and see value in it, besides nobody has to know if I enter it or not.

I decided to enter the competition and not tell anyone except two of my best friends. I decided only they could know because that way I wouldn't be embarrassed if I didn't make it. I didn't even tell Max because I knew he would think it was crazy and judge me, and I didn't want to be judged at that point. I needed strength, not insecurity. I actually felt very insecure about nominating myself for the competition and I knew he would have lots of questions about why I felt the need to do something so crazy. So I didn't tell him; I wasn't ready for his questions yet - I didn't really have any answers. I just felt a need to enter the competition.

I also wanted to enter the competition because I wanted to meet Ben Barry. Ben was one of the sponsors of the event and the grand prize was a one year modeling contract with his agency. Ben is responsible for the Dove Beauty Campaign. He convinced Dove to use "real people" as models in their beauty campaign and not typical size 0 models. I thought, hey, maybe I can be one of those girls. Maybe I can be the "Every Woman," I feel that I truly am just an average woman. Because I decided I wanted to meet Ben, I thought this competition could be a great way to get him to notice me. A burn survivor who is willing to get noticed as a model, now that I thought, was funny.

Who me, a model? Yeah right, never. As a kid, I didn't really like models. I always saw models as having a certain amount of arrogance. Who were they to think they were beautiful enough to be models? I was always taught that if you thought you were beautiful, you were pretty high on yourself and a bragger. I didn't realize how much skill and courage it took to get up on that runway until I did it.

I decided what the heck, I'll nominate myself for the competition, and who cares if I get in or not, let's just try it and see. Since no one knows, no harm done to my ego. Even Max won't be able to say anything if I don't get accepted because he won't know. And hey, maybe this is the Universe's way of giving me something I asked for. I asked the Universe for an opportunity to meet Ben Barry, maybe this was it.

At Christmas-time, Janeen and I decided to have a girls night out. I drove to Calgary, picked her up and we drove to Kananaskis to spend some quality girl-time in the hot tub, have a fabulous dinner, and walk in the mountains. What a great girls' evening.

We're in the hot tub and I say *"So, you want to hear the craziest thing I just did? I haven't told a single soul what I've done."* and she said *"Yes, of course, tell me."* I continued and said *"Well, this is absolutely the craziest thing I have ever done in my whole life, seriously."* She was already very curious because I've done some crazy things in my life and she's been around for most of them. I continued, *"Well, I nominated myself for a model search competition for the Every Woman Competition so I can meet Ben Barry."* And she just looked at me and said, *"You know you're going to get accepted don't you?"* And I said, *"Yep, I know. I know they're going to pick me and somehow I'm going to have to do this crazy thing."*

I think it was only one week later and I got an email saying congratulations, I had been accepted for the competition. I was one of 30-people selected out of 1500-nominees. I was SHOCKED beyond belief! I could not believe that they had actually paid attention to my nomination and selected me to participate. YIKES!!! Now what was I going to do? Seriously, me a model? No way.

Being a model went against everything I believed. I did not believe that I looked beautiful enough to be a model. I believed I had inner beauty, but definitely not the model quality outer beauty. But, that's where I was wrong. They weren't looking for the typical size zero woman to be the "Every Woman." They were looking for a "normal" woman. They were looking for a woman with strength and true beauty that shines from women who are confident and real. This whole event really played a lot with my inner head.

Following is my diary of the journey.

### Dear Diary (Sat, Mar 13)

*Today Catherine Vu and I drove down to Calgary for our dress fittings and hair appointments, then we're going to the runway practice tomorrow. I'm not sure how I'm going to feel about everyone dressing me up, but I'm just going to go with the flow and embrace this experience. It's not very often that I get to try on long gowns from Bellissima and high-end clothes from ChiChi Couture. I'm looking forward to being dressed by professionals. I know I'm definitely NOT going to like the runway practice, especially if he makes me walk in front of everyone. I know that's going to be the hard part for me. I'd rather do 10 more speeches than that.*

*Our first appointment was Bellissima, we met with June and she's such a darling. She's short, just like Catherine (she's 4'10") and it was so funny to see that I was the tall one of the bunch and I'm only 5'2". June made a rule that Catherine and I couldn't see what each other was trying on since we are both in the Top Ten and made us go in separate ends of the store. We just laughed about it because we don't see it as a competition against each other even though it is. We're just having fun and really happy that we have each other to share it with.*

*June and the other dress lady came over to me, held on to my arms and she said, "Kelly, I know you're a burn victim and is there anything you won't wear? Do you need to cover up yourself or can we just dress you up in anything?" I said, "Heck no, dress me up, I'll wear anything if it looks good! Heck, I'll even wear a bathing suit in public." Well, you should have seen those two girls, they jumped up and said, "That is so awesome, we just can't wait, we're going to have so much fun!" And then they put all the gowns in my dressing room. There was like 10 of them and most of them I would never pick for myself, but I was just going to go with the flow and see what looked great on me and trust their judgement. It was so funny watching the girls dress me up.*

*Each dress I tried on, they would instantly know whether it was good for me or not. I liked them all, but who am I, certainly not an expert in fashion. Then June said, "When you come out, we want to go WOW and if we don't, then we know it's the wrong dress for you." The funny part was when the customers walking by started saying "wow." That's when we knew we had the right dress. It finally came down to a long red mermaid-style dress and a short flowing blue one. I tried them both on twice and when more customers started watching and going "wow," we knew the blue one was the right choice.*

*As I was leaving the store, June gave me a hug and started crying. I asked her what was making her cry and she said that she was very proud of me for doing this and she hopes I win. She told me to strut my stuff and give it all I got so I can win it. I gave her another hug and had a great moment with her. People think I'm amazing for doing stuff like this, but I'm just ME! Anyways, off to the next fitting at ChiChi Couture.*

*We went to ChiChi Couture and they greeted us and were so excited to meet us and had outfits already designed and made for us. Holly, the owner/designer specially made outfits for us. At first, the clothes looked pretty plain, but apparently, once she decks us out with the jewellery before we get on the runway, we're going to look fantastic. She also said they're going to do our hair in Robert Palmer style all slicked back and heavy dark make-up around the eyes. Hmmmm, sounds interesting to me, not something I would normally do, but hey, I'm looking forward to the look and seeing if I can pull this off. I'm just going to go with the flow and trust them. I'm actually excited about it. I think it's going to be crazy fun.*

*Next, we're off to Edges Hair Salon, looking forward to having a high end stylist look after my hair. Not sure I like how short it is, but that's the great thing about hair, it grows and since professional stylists will be dressing me up and making me look great, I know they'll make sure I have great hair for the show. No more pony tails for a while!*

*So, we're done all our appointments for the day, and Catherine takes me to my best friend's house, Janeen. We have an amazing friendship and we just love each other so much and are so great for each other. She is one of my champions in my life. She knows me inside out, she knows what makes me tick and the great thing is she is one of few people who can be totally honest with me and I take it well. She tells me when I'm full of crap and when I'm truly being stupid and then she also tells me when to stop f%$#ing with my head and let me be the goddess I'm meant to be.*

*She always knows how to put me on the right path and gives me the energy and spirit I need to keep going. We always understand each other and if we don't, we figure it out. She's just one of those soulmate friends who I just love talking to and can't get enough of.*

**March 14, 2010 (Sun)**

*Today is the runway practice. I know this is going to be the hardest part for me. I really hope he doesn't make me walk in front of everyone, although I'm pretty positive he will. Have to make sure I bring my heels. I am really feeling insecure about this. I knew this was going to be a big part of the whole event, walking the runway, but man I wish I could somehow get out of this part. Do I really have to do this?*

*For the runway practice, a special coach was there teaching us how to walk. I don't know, how can a big man teach ladies how to walk? I don't get it. Anyways, it's all about feeling sexy and fabulous according to him and when I feel sexy and fabulous it will show on the runway. Hmmm, I have my doubts. For some reason none of that made me feel sexy or fabulous. This really is hard crap for me. I hated every minute of it. He made each of us (50 or so) stand in a circle around the edge of the room and then each of us had to take turns walking across the room and back.*

*We were supposed to state our name then say what we were uncomfortable about. Well, here's where my fearless voice just happened to shut right down and my fearful voice took right over. There was no way Fearless was going to win this battle! Jeepers, Fearless, take over damn it! You know I need you to win this battle if I'm ever going to think I can do this on the 20<sup>th</sup>. F\*#%! I have never in my life felt so uncomfortable and insecure in my whole life.*

*There were only about six girls ahead of me and Fearful was thinking of all kinds of things to do like, how about somehow getting to the back of the line and not the front? How about somehow faking sick and running out to the bathroom and staying there for the next hour. Something!!! Something, there has to be something I can do to get out of this. I always do well under pressure, but never during practice and don't make me do this in front of everyone! There is no way I can do this! There is no way I can walk out in front of everyone and have them all staring at me and judging me. All those girls who really want to be super models, let them be super models they can do this for me. I really don't need this attention. I really don't want this, what am I doing this for? Why? Really? Why? Why am I putting myself in this situation? I even texted my best friend and said, "I hate this f___n shit, why am I doing this?"*

*It came to my turn and the coach asked me my name and I told him and he asked me what I was uncomfortable about and I said that I can't do this in front of everyone. I can't walk in front of everyone here! I truly felt like crap, horrible and insecure. He encouraged me and said that I look fabulous and that I should feel fabulous and he's going to accept nothing less than fabulous from me.*

*And not only did I do it bad, he made me do it again because that's how bad I was the first time. Talk about pressure!*

*Although I know he was just trying to make me feel better, it didn't help me feel better at all. It gave me not one ounce of encouragement that's for sure. At that point, I felt I was going to lose the competition, there was no way I could win feeling that way. You could just see the girls who were having a great time with it and really did feel fabulous and sexy. Why didn't this make me feel that way? Why don't clothes or makeup or people telling me to feel sexy make me feel sexy? I don't get it and certainly don't understand what's going on. This isn't just about me doing this and meeting Ben Barry, this is about me facing this massive fear that I have of putting myself on display. I have spent my whole life avoiding the spotlight and now I was purposely exposing myself and **I felt naked with clothes on.***

*On the drive home, Catherine and I talked about it. She even told me that I looked uncomfortable walking in front of everyone. I asked her what is the difference between me standing on the stage speaking to people and walking down a runway and everyone staring at me? I have no problem speaking to people and they're staring at me, why is walking down a runway such a challenge for me? A very good question that I need to figure out so that I can wrap my head around this. Catherine figures I'm really not comfortable with my body like I think I am, it's just a little walk she said. Not to me, it was more than just a little walk.*

*So, I get home, decide to have a bath and Max and I have a talk. He tells me about his weekend and how much fun he had going out and I tell him about how great Saturday was with all the fittings and hair and then how crappy I felt on Sunday and I started to have a meltdown. I got a little annoyed with him because he proceeded to tell me that I didn't have to do this modeling thing in order to break into the speaking world and meet Ben Barry, there's other ways. I got really mad at him about it because I know he's wrong. This will be a fantastic way for me to get noticed by Ben and prove to myself that I can do this. I told him there's no way I'm quitting, I made top ten, I'm going all the way, I just need to get myself in the right head space to walk down that plank, either help me get into the right head space or not.*

### March 18, 2010

*Today, Janeen and I are working on developing a media list and a media advisory letter. I also got a brain wave that we should be contacting the disability magazines. I spent a lot of the day googling disability magazines. My story will also inspire people with disabilities and show them that if I can do this, so can they. We can't let our differences or disabilities stop us from achieving whatever it is we want in our lives. There's a place in this world for everyone, no matter whether you're able-bodied or disabled.*

*As I was growing up, I never even thought I could be a model. I always thought I wasn't beautiful enough and besides I hated being stared at, why would I want to draw more unnecessary attention to myself? What bothered me even more than the staring was the rejection. I knew that if I put myself out there that I wanted to be a model, I could face even more rejection. I was already dealing with tonnes of rejection as a kid, the last thing I needed was more people telling me no, I couldn't be a model because I wasn't pretty enough or tall enough or perfect enough. I already had enough rejection in my life, I didn't need any more.*

*I never saw myself as being a model and I even grew to hate the word. Even now when I tell my friends about what I'm doing, I find a way to avoid saying the "model" word. I don't see myself as a model at all, I see myself as just doing something crazy, throwing myself out there and seeing what happens.*

*I talked to Janeen at the end of the day and she informed me that she had just talked to Ben Barry. I said, "WHAT? How did that happen and is that all I had to do was just get you to phone him for me?" And she said, "Yep, but we didn't have a story before you decided to do this, now we do." Janeen had emailed him a copy of the media advisory so that he would be well aware of what was going on and that he may get some calls too. And any calls that she got for agency requests, she would forward on to him and she would handle any media requests for me. She is so smart! She just knows how to handle things.*

### March 19, 2010

*Dear Diary,*

*Today isn't THE day, but it might as well be because it sure feels like it. Today, Janeen and I are sending out the media advisory. We have everything planned, she's emailing them out by 8:30 a.m. and then whatever bounces back I'm faxing. She also needs me to print up a gazillion business cards (yep, she said a gazillion) plus she also needs 50 media advisories printed up and guess what??? My laptop won't work. The power connector somehow is pushed into the computer and my cable won't plug in properly. Crap!! What am I going to do now?*

*Good thing we bought the kids netbook computers for Valentine's day, 3 backups, yay! But, none of them are set up for printing so now I have to download printer drivers plus my business card file is on my broken laptop so I need to re-create them because I don't have anything on my son's computer. And the media advisory is also on my old laptop. Thank goodness for the internet and me having the picture for my business card plus the media advisory uploaded to my server. It's just time consuming redoing everything. Ugh! And plus Janeen wants me to be following up and making sure everyone got our media advisory that we sent today. Oh yeah, and of course I haven't started packing yet.*

*Got another call from Fashion Has No Borders and they wanted to congratulate me again for making top ten and wondered who's clothes I'm modeling for the Top Ten competition. They then called back and told me that the Top Ten competition will be just like a beauty pageant competition and we'll have to model the clothes plus the judges will be asking us questions again. The question part doesn't bother me, I'm good at that, but I still have this fear of walking the plank. Hey, maybe I'll be like that model on America's Top Model and fall down the stairs and then get knocked off the plank. Hey head!!!! Shut up! I have to keep telling my Fearful inner voice to shut up and take a hike so my Fearless voice can take over. What a lot of head games my head is playing with me. Wow! I have never had so much crap go on in my*

139

*head. The fear and stress is really starting to settle in and of course I just HAD to wake up to three cold sores, not one, but three! For two weeks I have been putting lysine on to prevent them from coming and I got one last week, trying to get that to go away then developed another one and then the third one came on my upper lip this a.m. Why can't lip stuff live up to its name?*

*So, I'm starting to feel the stress and wondering what the f&#% am I doing this for? Is it really going to be worth it? Absolutely, I just love it when my Fearless voice takes over – she won't even let me think about quitting. My Fearful inner voice just takes a back seat on that one – I think she secretly believes that Fearless is actually right on this one, but she still likes to sneak in her shots here and there and put in the self doubt. But ultimately my Fearless voice is winning this battle.*

*Janeen has been emailing like crazy getting all sorts of responses and people wanting interviews and pictures. We're both happy about the success we're having. So far, nobody has said no. Janeen is so awesome and I love that she's doing this for me. I know she can sell me and tell my story better than me. She just sees how awesome I am, I just see me as being me – crazy me. The me who just likes to see if she can accomplish something else that somebody said she couldn't do. And this one is a big one. I have to say that I see this as the biggest thing ever.*

### March 20, 2010

*Dear Diary,*

*Today is THE day. Today is the day that I take the stage and let all the girls fuss over me and do my hair and make-up (even though I hate that part), dress me up and put me on the runway to walk the plank. I'm not sure if I can do this, but I'm not quitting. Fearless is going to win the battle of me at least walking the plank. It won't be easy for sure, but I will do it. I'm not a quitter and I have gone way too far to quit now.*

*Just a little disappointed, found out that Ben Barry won't be able to make it – he had a death in the family. So sorry for Ben, that is sad. Death is very terrible and reminds me of just a few short months ago when my Dad died. Time to go and be a model for a day. Yay! Not!*

**March 21, 2010**

*Dear Diary,*

*Today I am glad everything is all over with. I didn't win the title of Every Woman, but I did win the Twitter People's Choice Award. Yay! I have to remember to thank Janeen and Karen for helping me win, it was their idea to get everyone to vote on Twitter. I'm glad I can put this all behind me and be done with it. I have some great stories to tell if I ever decide to write a book.*

*I was so glad my cousin Rod and his wife Brenda came to watch me at the finals. It meant a lot to me to have them there. One reason I was hoping to win was so that I could tell everyone the reason I got burnt and not him was because this was the "Every Woman" competition, not the "Every Man" competition. He would have loved that.*

*I can't believe Tamara from the Mom Magazine and her husband drove all the way to Calgary just to cheer me on. I remember hearing her – she was fantastic and it made me feel so good that she wanted to be there for me.*

*Of course, Max and the kids were there too along with Janeen, her man Bill and his daughter, Karen. I didn't realize how great it would make me feel having them all there to support me.*

*The only thing that would have made the event even better was having my Mom, Don, Kim, Tim and Abbey there, but they're all in Arizona, but that's ok because Kim came to round one and I totally appreciate that.*

*I was a little disappointed because I really thought I would win the big prize and be able to meet Ben Barry and really get to know him and what he stands for. I really feel that we can do some speaking together.*

*Although I did feel better walking the plank yesterday than when we had our runway practice, I know that being a model would be a very difficult thing for me to do. In a way, I'm actually glad that I didn't win the competition. I would have had to be a model for a year with Ben and maybe I wouldn't be able to live up to his expectations.*

*My friend Lynda (who is also a burn survivor) put a great comment on my Facebook status. She said although you didn't win the big money prize, the people picked you and it's the people's opinion that counts most. Her comment made me feel great because she's right, the people wanted me to win and that's the best part.*

### March 23, 2010

*Dear Diary,*

*Wow! The media is going nuts for my story – they just love that a burn victim won a beauty pageant and has discovered her beauty from within and faced her fear of walking the plank in front of everyone. And how she put herself on display after avoiding the spotlight for all her life. And how amazing is it that she also has a husband, daughter and twin sons oh yeah and don't forget, her business too.*

*We have 13-media requests and it looks like another trip back to Calgary is in order. Global Television wants to do a story and they want me to bring my daughter too. CTS TV also wants to do an interview, along with CBC and CTV. Oh yeah, and the Edmonton Examiner wants to do a story and some other prominent magazines. Wow! This is all fantastic great stuff. Who would have thought my story would create all this media?*

I realized that when the Universe throws you a bone, you have to take it. I asked the Universe for an opportunity to meet Ben Barry and sure enough I found the Every Woman Competition on Facebook. If I wouldn't have acted on it, I would have sent a message back to the Universe that I really didn't want to meet Ben. That was a message from the Universe giving me an opportunity I was looking for. Yes, this event put me out of my comfort zone and when I acted on what the Universe provided me with, I ended up receiving a tonne of rewards that I didn't expect. *"Thank you Universe, for giving me these opportunities to face my fear and inspire others."*

Another example showing the power of possibilities is a story by another great friend, Candace. When I met Candace for the first time, she responded to an advertisement I had about a scrapbooking garage sale. She came over with her kids and she just had this amazing personality. She was bubbly right from the moment I met her, and she had such a cool sense of humor, I just knew that I wanted to be her friend. Candace got her friends attending a monthly Girls Night Out Club with me and my mobile scrapbook store and we have been friends ever since.

One day she started to tell me about her past and I was quite shocked that someone so amazing could have such a traumatic past, so I asked her to write about it. She had such a positive and amazing attitude that I couldn't see her being the traumatized kid she told me about, all I could see was a women going places. Following is Candace's story.

*Dear Kelly,*

*I grew up in a very dysfunctional environment, where trafficking drugs, abusing substances, and negativity were a part of everyday life. What is a kid to do with an abundance of unhealthy role models, including a father serving time for second-degree murder?*

*How did I get from being this kid with everything against me, to a healthy, drug-free, successful business owner, loving wife, and adoring mother? I believed in possibilities, I also believed in myself. I knew I deserved more and I made good choices in life. I chose not to feel sorry for myself, and dwell on the negative. I chose to be grateful, and positive, and in return life opened a door of never ending possibilities & opportunities which led me to be the happy, fulfilled, thankful individual I am today.*

*Never accept defeat, or poor circumstances. Turn it around by believing in the possibility of dreams coming true. People still ask me how I managed to turn out so good, especially my Dad who is amazed by my attitude toward life and my ability to rise above circumstance. My answer to them is simple, anything is possible.*

*By Candace Robichaud*

# REJECTION

## Facing the Fear of Rejection

One of my friends told me that he fears rejection, so much so that he would rather see an opportunity pass by than take the chance and get a yes. He said that he's too scared to flirt with a lady because he fears she will reject him. This confused me, because what if he would have got a yes? But no, he automatically fears that she will reject him. I told him he's crazy and that he shouldn't be so hard on himself - he has tons going for him and he's a great guy. I reminded him that if he doesn't start flirting he's never going to find a woman to fall in love with him and make him happy.

Let's be real. I'm the Queen of Rejection - I have probably faced more rejection in my life than most people have, but I don't let it stop me. I always assume I'm going to get the positive or the yes that I want and if they reject me, I just blow it off with an *'oh well,'* then on to the next opportunity. If it is something I really want, I fight for it. I fight for what I want until there's absolutely no other way.

Why do people fear rejection? Do they get scared of that little pain that their ego feels? If you don't go for it, you will never know if you could have gotten the "YES." What about the joy you could feel? Besides, even if you get a "NO" what's going to happen to you? Yeah, you'll feel a little bit of a hurt ego, but there are millions of people in the world who could say "YES," and I would rather take the risk and get the joy than worry about a little pain in my ego.

One time, I found out, there was a horseback riding judge who couldn't even judge me when I was competing in horse shows because she couldn't look past my scars. There was no way I was going to let her insecurities stop me from doing what I loved at the time. I kept on competing and eventually I started winning prizes. If I would have given up, I wouldn't have won the prizes. I believed in myself and didn't want to give up; I wanted to succeed. Her opinion did not matter to me. I knew only I mattered to me and I wasn't going to give up my passion for riding horses for her. She was only one judge and her opinion only counted one time.

At school dances, guys wouldn't ask me to dance so I would ask them. Yes, I was turned down many times, in fact, almost always, but I kept trying because I knew eventually someone would have the courage to say yes. If I would have let all those guys bring me down, I would have never made it to be the woman I am today. If I'd had let all those rejections knock me down, I also never would have found Max. I met Max in a bar and I believe he actually did turn me down once, but the next time he didn't. hehe

**Rejection** - I know it's tough to handle, but the tougher rejection for me is when my inner Fearful voice is talking. When I doubt myself, I try to tell my inner Fearful voice to take a hike and let my inner Fearless voice take over.

## Friend Rejection

One day, in Elementary school, my best friend decided to hang out with the bully in school and not me. He was my best friend and crush from kindergarten to grade five. He used to bring me pencils and I used to save up pennies so he could buy books from the book club. I also used to share my cookies with him, every day since kindergarten until one day in grade-five. My best friend and the bully came up to me. My best friend said, "I don't want to be your friend any more, you've been in all my classes and I don't like it and I don't want to be your friend." This was the last day I talked to him for 38-years.

The rejection always bothered me because he was my best friend for six years (our moms were even friends) and I could never understand how he could dump me for the bully. This was the bully who would pick on me and call me scar-face and draw pictures of me with scribbles all over my face and was just generally very mean to me. I had a hard time understanding it, because he was mine and my protector, not the bullies'. He belonged to me and he did for six years, how could he leave me now? This was one fight I walked away from. I didn't fight for him, I let him go and I regret that decision. I should have made him be my friend, but he was just a dumb 10-year old boy trying to fit with the bully. He didn't realize he was hurting me. And I don't think he really thought he would lose his daily supply of cookies either.

I decided to take on the challenge of organizing our 25-year school reunion with some other friends. I did it because there were three people I wanted there, and he was one of them. I felt this was my purpose and reason for ending the silent treatment. I had a reason to call him and make sure he knew about the reunion and see him.

One of my other fun tasks was to find out about people's secret crushes, so I asked him who his secret crush was in high school. He gave me a name and then said that he still had a crush on her and I laughed. Then I asked him, jokingly, *"So what grade was your crush on me?"* And he said, *"Right up until the day you quit sharing your cookies with me."* I cracked up and laughed so hard! I couldn't believe it!

Two things happened for me. First, I realized he was the only guy ever to admit that he had a crush on me in school and second, I realized that he still remembered us back in grade-five. Then he said, *"Yep, always remember the good things in life."* I had a huge smile on my face and it brought back a lot of great memories, rather than focusing on the bad ones.

Eventually, we met. I brought a box of cookies and asked him if he wanted to share cookies with me again. He laughed and then we talked for hours. We had a lot of catching up to do; 38-years worth of it. The conversation was great, and then somehow we started talking about the day he stopped being my friend, the day I stopped sharing my cookies. He didn't remember the story and felt tremendous guilt for doing what he did. He apologized profusely and asked me why I didn't kick him. He did not want to end our friendship at all; he was just being a dumb 10-year old boy and his friendship with the bully was very short.

Anyways, this situation made me realize that friendships are worth fighting for, and that I really should have kicked him, told him he was being dumb, and then told him that if he didn't smarten up he wouldn't have any more cookies. I can't believe he gave up his daily supply of cookies for the bully in class! The best part is that I've totally forgiven him and we are great friends again! Take that Bully!

## Model Search Rejection

When I heard about the Every Woman Competition I thought about the potential rejection I could feel. What if they didn't want to accept my nomination? What if they rejected me like so many other people had? What if I wasn't good-looking enough to be in the model search? I handled the potential rejection by not telling anyone about the competition, and nominating myself instead of asking someone else to. I knew my ego could handle the rejection as long as nobody knew about the crazy thing I had done.

When they accepted my nomination and told me I was one of 30 selected out of 1500-women, I started to tell people, but even then I still didn't tell a lot of people. I waited until I competed in round one and won a spot in the Top Ten. Once I made the top ten, I wasn't worried about the rejection any more. I knew that my inner fearless voice had taken over and was winning that battle. The next step was to compete in the finals and that was where I won the Twitter Peoples' Choice Award. I didn't win the big money prize, but I won the next best thing, and that made me feel great! In fact, I felt even greater, because I won an award that was the people's choice, people who said they wanted me to win, and that meant more to me.

The moral of this story is, if I would have let the fear of rejection get in my way, I never would have nominated myself and I never would have won the Twitter Peoples' Choice Award and I wouldn't be able to inspire millions of people with my "Beauty from Within" story. I'm glad that I'm able to inspire others to look within themselves and see their true authentic beauty.

**My advice:** quit fearing rejection and embrace success - who knows, you just may get success. I believed in me, and success is what I have.

## Physical Attraction

When I went to school, one thing I always wanted, but never had was a boyfriend. All my friends had them, but for me it was different because I had scars. Because I was different, it was hard for guys to step out of their comfort zone and take the risk of being judged by their friends. I still had those crushes and a lot of times it was hard for me to accept that the guys didn't like me in that way. I always had a lot of friends who were guys, but none of them would take that next step and be my boyfriend. They always wanted the pretty girl, not the scar-faced girl.

When I was in high school, I used to wear the tightest jeans ever. I used to need a clothes hanger to pull up my zipper. There was one guy I was really hoping to impress; he was my secret crush in grade-12. I found out 24-years later, that he still remembered my "hot ass, in my tight jeans." I laughed when I found out that the guy I was trying to impress was impressed, but we were both too shy to act on it. But I was also really mad at him for waiting that long to tell me. I wanted the attention back in high school, not now.

It took me many years to figure out why guys weren't interested in me in school. It's all about physical attraction and if you're not attracted to someone physically, you can't develop that deep emotional bond with them that is needed to have an exciting long-lasting relationship. I totally understand why the guys that I liked or had crushes on didn't like me the way I liked them; they weren't physically attracted to me, and it wasn't their fault. Attraction is not something you can control or choose. It's either there or it's not.

Once I finished high school, all of a sudden finding guys wasn't as much of an issue. I think it was because high school was all about boundaries and fitting in. I met Max, my husband when I was 19, and he wasn't scared to admit that he was attracted to me. We've been together ever since. Never give up because there is always the possibility that things could change and you will eventually find your happiness.

I'll never forget the day Max took me, his best friend and his sister to Calgary to meet his oldest brother. The five of us were walking around and his brother said, *"Max, what's wrong with this girl, she's beautiful, why don't you marry her?"* He was talking about me! And then I remember Max turning around, looking at me and saying, *"You know what, I just might marry her."* and gave me his big winning smile. I just laughed and said, *"Yeah right, we'll see about that."* At that time I had only known Max for a couple months, so I wasn't thinking about marriage at all.

I'm glad I now understand what physical attraction is. Physical attraction is a two-way street. You both have to be attracted to each other in order to make it work. I just didn't find the guy who was attracted to me in high school. I found him, and now I've been in this relationship for 24-years.

When I was younger, I used to feel guilty because my girlfriends, who had more experience with guys when we were teenagers, were still struggling to find the man of their dreams while I had been in my relationship for over five years. I used to wonder how come my beautiful girlfriends couldn't find someone to settle down with, but yet here was me, no experience; no prior relationship; now in a long-term stable one? Hmmm, really, I still don't have the answer to that one.

**My advice:** Don't be so hard on yourself if someone doesn't like you enough to be your boyfriend or girlfriend; they just might not be attracted to you and it's not your fault. Find the one who is attracted to you, your relationship will be way more satisfying and will last longer.

## Amazing People

When people hear my story and everything I've accomplished, they think I'm so amazing and I always find that funny because I don't think I'm that amazing. I think my friends are just as amazing as I am. I think everyone has amazing stories; it's just that some choose to tell them and others choose to keep them in.

I think people say I'm amazing because I'm a burn survivor and I've done so many things in my life. People just expect that since I'm a victim of a traumatic burn injury that I would just quit life. I wasn't given an option to quit life.

While some people think I'm amazing, I think I'm just ME. That's right, just ME and the best me that I can be. So many times I thought something was wrong with me because I do so many things, but there's nothing wrong with me, I love to accomplish things. I've done a million things and I know I'll do a million more.

Life is full of things to do. When something inspires me, I find a way to do it. Even though I wasn't considered one of the "pretty girls," I still tried out for the cheerleading squad, I still tried out for choir, I still asked the guys to dance, and I still put myself out there because I knew that I wouldn't get anywhere in life if I just stayed home and continued to be shy and blamed everything on my scars. Eventually people started saying to me that they didn't notice my scars, they noticed my inner beauty.

People often assume that because I am burnt, I would be this shy insecure girl, but I'm not. I used to be. When I was in school I was shy, but then I also realized that I was missing out on opportunities in life. I realized that some times I was going to face rejection and I was going to have my pride hurt, but what was more important to me was not letting myself down and letting others get in my way of what I wanted in life.

I was being teased by bullies, and at one time even called "Scarface." I'll never forget this one bully, Kelly, (pretty funny, we both have the same name) he was a big, big guy and I knew that if I walked by him, he was going to say something rude and nasty. I remember one day I saw him, and knew the only way to get where I wanted to go was to walk past him. I remember saying to myself, *"ok, here he is, just walk by, ignore him and hopefully he won't see you."* He made his comment as I was walking by, but what I didn't know was that one of my friends, Todd, was walking behind me and heard the bully make the rude comment. Well, this time he wasn't getting away with it. Todd blasted him first and then I took a round out of him and together we got the bully kicked out of school. I still remember Todd saying that he should pick on someone his own size and definitely not a girl. I was so thankful that Todd was there sticking up for me. It was nice to see that I wasn't the only one tired of watching me get teased.

Ultimately, I had to learn to accept that I was going to be stared at and a lot of times teased and I had to learn how to deal with the teasing and staring. Every time it was different. Some times I wanted to be nice and other times I just wanted to make a rude comment back. There were other times I just wanted to turn away so they couldn't get a second or third look. I've learned over the years, that some times they're not staring at me because they think I'm ugly, but because I'm cute, beautiful, hot and/or sexy. Beauty comes from within, and I found that when I dress great, I felt great, and then people don't notice my scars. People start noticing my inner beauty; and that's me, the best me I can be!

One time I went to the bar with some friends and I asked my buddy, Paul, to walk me back to my car. We were at the mall, it was dark outside and I didn't want to walk by myself, so of course Paul, being the gentleman he is said he would walk me. As we were walking, we both noticed some guy staring at me and I happened to make a comment like, jeepers creepers another person staring at me. Paul looked at me and said, *"He's staring at you because you're so darn cute."* I just chuckled, gave him the look and said, *"Yeah right Paul"* and we kept walking.

A few years later I started thinking about that night and I thought to myself, why couldn't someone be thinking I'm cute? Why do I always assume that when someone is staring at me, that I think they're thinking I'm ugly? When I stare at people, I don't always think the worst or the negative, there's a lot of times when I look at someone and I think, wow, that person looks great. I don't always think the negative, so why can't people be thinking the same as me? Why can't people be thinking, wow, she's got scars, but she's still beautiful?

**That was when I realized that I had to stop thinking that every time someone is staring at me, they're thinking I'm ugly. I had to stop caring about what others thought of me and caring about what I thought of me.** Seriously, was I ever going to see them again? And really, did their opinions really matter? NO! I didn't need to be concerned with their opinions because they didn't matter in my world, just like the garage sale lady didn't matter to me. I didn't need any more clutter in my head, so now when someone stares at me, I choose to ignore it with a smile.

Following is a letter that I wrote to Sharon Cornwall, the owner and show producer from Fashion Has No Borders. A few months after the competition, I realized why walking the plank was so difficult for me and I explained it in this letter to Sharon.

*Dear Sharon,*

*Thank you for choosing me to be one of the top 30 to compete in the Every Woman Competition. When I decided to nominate myself for this event, I really had to evaluate "if" and "why" I wanted to do this event. Growing up as a young burn survivor I never felt "beautiful" enough to be a model. It took a lot of courage for me to enter in to this event, but I did it because I wanted a chance to prove to myself that I could do it and even more so I wanted to meet Ben Barry. I didn't tell anyone that I nominated myself for this event except for two of my best friends. I didn't even tell my husband because I didn't want to answer to anyone about why I did something so crazy that I would normally never do.*

*When I was selected to compete, I was overjoyed and wildly excited because finally someone thought I was beautiful enough to compete in a model search competition. I knew I would do good with the speeches because speaking doesn't bother me, but I was more concerned with walking the runway or "the plank" as I call it in my story. At the time, I didn't know why walking the plank would be so difficult for me until months later.*

*When I walked the plank, it took me back to a very dark part in my life. It took me back to my childhood when I would have to walk in front of all the non-burn kids and I knew they were whispering about me, teasing me and calling me names like the ugly scar-faced girl. And although when I walked the plank for your event, I knew people weren't saying those things about me, it still took me back to that time when I was a kid and felt so insecure walking in front of them.*

*I am very glad I competed in the Every Woman Competition for a number of reasons, but mostly because it made me conquer my fear of walking the plank and realize what my fear was. When you organized that modeling practice where we had to learn how to walk as a model,*

*I was going through some major issues in my head. My inner Fearless voice had shut right down and my inner Fearful voice had taken right over. There was even a point where I was going to fake being sick and somehow get out of walking in front of all those girls and "real" models. When I got home, I told my husband about it, had a meltdown and said I needed his help to get my head in the right frame of mind to finish the competition. I knew I wouldn't quit because I had too much to gain and nothing to lose but a hurt ego.*

*As hard as it was for me to walk that plank, I still did it, knowing that somehow my inner Fearless self would take over and help me do it. And I did. And I am forever grateful for nominating myself. Although I didn't get to meet Ben Barry in person, he is now following me on twitter and we have developed an online friendship and some day we will meet. As a result of winning this award, I have been on radio shows, television episodes, have stories in various women magazines, newspapers and online magazines. Not only did I gain major media and publicity, this event has been a great launch to my keynote speaking career – I have discovered that my true story is about discovering the "Beauty from Within" and "No Risks, No Rewards." I also sent my Social Media Release (Burn Victim Survivor Walks the Plank Wins the Award and Lives to Tell the Story) to an online media service and my story got picked up by over 100 other internet media and organizations. Now I also have my own radio show on the WIN Network, plus I recently won the "Fierce Woman of the Year 2010" award from the Mom Magazine.*

*So yes, I am very grateful that I decided to take the risk, nominate myself and reap all the rewards from this event. Although I didn't win the big money prize and meet Ben Barry, the people wanted me to win and that is what mattered the most to me and ultimately, I proved to myself that I could face my fear and walk that plank and prove to myself that I am truly beautiful even with scars on 75% of my body.*

*Thank you again, Sharon, for putting on this very real and fantastic event. More people need to know that they are real women who deserve to be recognized too.*

*Kelly Falardeau*

## NO RISK, NO REWARDS

*If you don't take the risk – there's no chance of you ever getting the reward – the failure rate is HUGE! -- Kelly*

**Ultimately, life is about choices.** You can choose to be happy or you can choose to be sad. You can choose to feel ugly or you can choose to feel beautiful. You can choose to believe that people are staring at you because they think you're ugly or you can choose to think that people think you're beautiful or just curious about what happened. You can choose to follow your dreams or you can choose to feel sorry for yourself because others get their dreams and you don't. You can choose to walk out that door no matter what others think or you can choose to hide inside because you think you don't deserve a life.

I choose life. I deserve life just like anyone else whether I have scars or not. I choose to walk out that door whether I'm in a bathing suit or wearing pig tails or wearing a business suit. I choose to follow my dreams. I choose to find my passions in life. I choose to feel happy. I choose to find the good in situations instead of dwelling on all the bad. I choose to not care if someone else stares at me or comments about my scars. I choose to feel great about ME. I give myself permission to be all that and more because I want to live, dream and prosper. And ultimately, I also believe that anyone can have what they want if they choose life.

I love this story from my friend Laura – she talks about how she did such crazy things in order to get the reward of being able to say "I did it."

*Dear Kelly,*

*I am a woman*
*I am a mother*
*I am a wife*
*I am a friend*
*I am a daughter*

*I am a sister*
*I want to be me.*

*I feel the responsibilities of life have taken a piece of who I once was. They have taken my last name, my independence, my spontaniaty, and most of all my uniqueness. My uniqueness is the one that I miss the most. The part of me that seems to have vanished like my perky boobs.*

*My life's ambition is.... to find ME.*

*The one that will do anything, the one that will try anything, and live in the moment. The one that worked on the railway swinging a hammer, or lived in a Atco trailer in the Northern Ontario bush with 35-men and drove a hi-rail, just for the experience of it. Sleeping outside a coliseum to get Garth Brooks tickets, just to say I did it.*

*The same girl that dropped a 50-pound keg of nails on her breast (longer story than is allowed), got poison ivy on my rear end from having to suddenly take cover when trying to pee discretely in the bush away from the railway track.*

*The one that was proud to be one of the few women that worked out on the railroad track crews and pulled her weight, not to mention made things interesting. The girl that thinks of experiences in story telling degrees.....over drinks story, with select people stories, and tell your grandchildren stories.*

*I do not regret my responsibilities in any of those other roles. They are stories that I will tell when I am old and gray.......er. I want to build on them, including them.*

*As a mother, I have to work hard every day to be the mother I always wanted to be; the one that I saw in my mind and took inventory of. The qualifications of the mother that everyone wants to have that I had created in my immature mind; which I have sadly fallen short of, but I have a goal and that is the first step!*

*As a wife I have to learn as I go. Always learning; always bending and changing. Sometimes the bending and changing is more painful than others, and sometimes to be successful it requires karma sutra techniques, but as they say "no pain, no gain." The other roles challenge me to adjust to who needs me and for what at that time. In all the changing, I have lost track of who I was, me....Laura Featherstone and maybe just maybe one day she will be found.*

By Laura Featherstone

This story is from my friend Annette Stanwick, she talks about a different kind of reward, forgiveness.

Dear Kelly,

*My brother Soren had been brutally murdered in 1999. We had so many unanswered questions like: Who had killed him and why? Grief recovery wasn't easy, but I made 3 very important choices. Number one, I made the choice to be happy again. Number two, I didn't want to be consumed by Soren's death; and number three I made the choice to grow in spite of what had happened. Even though I'd made those 3 choices, I had no idea what they would look like or where those choices would take me.*

*Throughout the recovery period, I did a lot of reading, praying, weeks in grief counseling in addition to lots of writing. My motorcycle also became an instrument of healing and opportunity to process my pain during the many hours of solitude on long trips. Those times of solitude and deep introspection helped me realize I didn't have a choice in what happened to my brother, but I truly had a choice in how I would respond to what had happened. I also experienced some tremendous revelations on board my motorcycle that ked me to make other choices that were transformational on my healing journey.*

*After my brother's murderer was found, he confessed, so there would be no trial, but my other family members and I were invited to attend the sentencing of the one who'd taken his life and we were invited to present Victim Impact Statements. At the conclusion of my statement I made one more very important choice. I took a huge risk! Would my family members misunderstand what I was about to do? Would they alienate me? I made the choice to offer forgiveness to my brother's murderer! Forgiveness did not excuse or erase the harm that had been done, but forgiveness released me from the chains of anger, resentment and bitterness that could have controlled me for a very long time-even the rest of my life. Yes, I took a huge risk that day, but I received a great reward! My brother's murderer went away to serve the rest of his life in prison, but I came away a free woman! My family members accepted and loved me even though they hadn't come to the point of forgiveness in their own healing journey.*

*Annette Stanwick*
*International Speaker, Global Freedom Facilitator and*
*Award-winning Author of FORGIVENESS:*
*THE MYSTERY AND MIRACLE*
*www.annettestanwick.com*

# THE CURRENT DAY

So, what's up in my current life? I feel very blessed that I have gone from feeling like the insecure, ugly scar-faced girl to being a strong, married woman with three beautiful kids and having some of the greatest friends and family. I feel blessed with having discovered that my passion in life is being a speaker and spreading my message.

My kids constantly remind me to not sweat the little stuff and I'm always reminding myself that it's just a "little thing" and not worth getting upset about.

I still remember telling Max I wanted to follow my passion and be a speaker. He said to me, *"How are you going to do that?"* And I said, *"I don't know, but it will happen."* And now, all these wonderful things have started happening to me that I am totally grateful for and now I know that I can't quit.

Once I decided to follow my passion in life and become a speaker and share my message, tremendous things have been happening to me. I won the Twitter Peoples' Choice Award at the Fashion Has No Borders Every Woman Competition, I've been featured in some major media, I've been asked to host my own radio show, I also won the Fierce Woman of the Year Award by the Mom Magazine and I'm in demand as a keynote speaker on **"Finding Your Beauty From Within"** as well as **"No Risks, No Rewards."**

Follow your passion, because it's true that when you do and you're in alignment with your passion, nothing but greatness will follow and it doesn't feel like work.

# Here's What I Know

I thought I would end this book with my random thoughts about what I've learned over the course of my life.

I know that:

- Life is too short and too precious to be miserable
- I am not perfect and neither is anyone else in this world
- Perfection is highly overrated and unachievable, but near perfect is good enough for me
- I may not be the perfect writer, but I do know how to handle staring and teasing
- Beauty is more than just your outer looks, it's your inner looks that count
- You need to pick your battles, life is too short to get upset because someone didn't do the dishes or put the cap on the toothpaste
- It really doesn't matter how beautiful someone else thinks you are because only your opinion counts most
- When people stare, they aren't always thinking I'm ugly, they could be thinking I'm beautiful, hot or sexy, or they could be thinking, what happened to her?
- Only you can make yourself feel beautiful, not any one else
- Life is for the living, I can choose to be a victim and hide, or I can choose to live and be a survivor. I choose to live
- I'm a survivor, a fighter, a believer
- I deserve to feel beautiful no matter what others think and so do you
- Life is full of opportunities, abundance and possibilities, you just need to ask the Universe for what you want
- I have done a million things and will do a million more
- I love inspiring people to feel great about themselves
- I love helping people to discover their true beauty from within
- I will never give up on something I believe in no matter how long it takes
- I believe the Universe will provide me with what I need when I need it
- Everything happens for a reason, I just don't know what that reason is all the time, but eventually I find it out
- I can achieve anything if I want it bad enough

- I believe that if you want something, you should go get it
- The Universe has great things planned for everyone, it just takes time for the Universe to put the details in place
- I am not any more amazing than any one else, I just don't let my scars stop me from getting what I want
- Nobody is going to just give it to me, I have to go and get it
- If I don't ask, I'll never receive; if you don't ask, you'll never receive either
- Dreams are meant to be "found" not tucked away in Dreamland
- When you have found your passion in life and you're in alignment, everything just falls into place easily
- We all need Champions and Heroes in our lives to help us get through the rough times, find yours
- There is a good and a bad to everything, I choose to find the good in things
- If you don't take the risk, you will never receive the reward, you will have a 100% failure rate

## To book me as a speaker:

Check out my website at: www.mykellyf.com

My blog: http://blog.mykellyf.com

Check out this short movie, I'm in it: *(Thanks Tracy Matthewman for including me, this is awesome!)*

http://theanythingmovie.com/

# Advertisers

## Canadian Scrapbooker

My favorite scrapbooking magazine:
www.canadianscrapbooker.ca

## R & R Scrapbooking

My favorite place to buy scrapbooking supplies online:
www.scrapbooking.ca

## Eyes to the Sole Beauty & Wellness

I am a Reflexology practitioner through Eyes to the Sole Beauty & Wellness also providing facial treatments, cellulite treatments, and Ionic foot baths, treating you from head to toe. I am also a beauty and wellness consultant with Nu Skin Enterprises. Coming soon, Reiki treatments. Please visit me at Look forward to serving you!

**Laurette Wilvers 780.739.5550**
www.eyestothesole.com and www.laurettewilvers.nsedreams.com

## Roots & Wings Imagery

Roots & Wings Imagery depicts my life and what I am most passionate about; my boys; family; friends; and life in its entirety. I love to capture and nurture the memories I find through my lens for you to keep. My pictures dictate how Rooted my world is from the love of the land, critters and the simplistic lifestyle and the freedom to grow Wings to explore the endless possibilities that await.

**Kelly Walton (780) 231-3169**
rootsandwingsimagery@gmail.com

# The Bad Kitty

Christie Mawer is The Bad Kitty. She used to be a shy girl who lived in fear of even opening her mouth, let alone pursuing her dreams. Christie conquered her insecurities and learned to live by being true to herself. Now she supports other women to embrace their own uniqueness—including the fun and mischievous Bad Kitty within. As a speaker and dance instructor, through sensual dance and personal development, Christie seeks to give every woman the gift of self-acceptance by living the motto, "Be Beautiful, Be YOU!"

**AS A SPECIAL GIFT TO NO RISK, NO REWARDS READERS, Christie would like to offer you a FREE SENSUALITY COACHING SESSION** (1/2 hour, $75 value) and a COPY OF HER EBOOK (10 Ways You're a Bad Kitty Already – Even If You Don't Know It - $15 Value)   * sensuality coaching   * inspirational speaker   * sensuality workshops   * pole dancing home parties and classes

**Christie Mawer  780-893-9754**
Christie@TheBadKitty.com
www.TheBadKitty.com

# Online PR Media

Online PR Media is the place where traditional media press releases are supercharged with multimedia, social media, and search engine optimization -- to give you the most visibility for your news releases. Our SEO press releases, multimedia press releases, and newswire press release distribution put your news in front of the right people at the right time.
http://www.onlineprmedia.com/

**Tara Geissinger**
www.onlineprmedia.com

# About Kelly

**Kelly Falardeau is an author, entrepreneur and a motivational speaker.**

Friends, family and those who have worked with Kelly all say that Kelly doesn't let fear stop her – when she wants to achieve something, she just does it. They also say that the fact that Kelly is a burn survivor since she was two years old is so motivating because she does not let circumstances dictate her success.

At 21, she was nominated and won the position of President of the Alberta Burn Rehabilitation Society. As a kid, she also won the 4-H Most Improved Member award plus various public speaking awards and even the fastest senior typist award in high school.

Kelly has been featured on TV in Canada such as Global TV Edmonton and Calgary, CTS TV, CTV TV, Breakfast TV, Access TV, CBC, A-Channel and CFRN. She has also appeared as a guest on a various radio shows too. Articles have been written about her in the Edmonton Woman Magazine, Edmonton Examiner, Edmonton Journal, Edmonton Sun, Pioneer Balloons Balloon Magazine and she also won the MOM Executive Officer award from the Mom Magazine.

Kelly was chosen amongst thousands to present her business to the Dragons for the Dragons' Den television series plus won the "Fierce Woman of the Year 2010" award. Kelly was selected out of 1500-women to compete in the Every Woman model search competition, sponsored by Fashion Has No Borders. She faced her fear of being judged by her appearance and walked the runway and won the Peoples' Choice award.

She is a sought-after international speaker because of her ability to engage others. She is able to move audience's emotions and make them see how a bad situation can become a great one. She will have you crying, laughing and dancing in your chairs as she shares her many stories about 'No Risks, No Rewards'.

Kelly also speaks about the 'Beauty from Within' and how she faced her fear of walking the plank and discovered her true beauty. Her "beauty" exercise is a dynamite experience that shows teenagers and adults where their true beauty comes from.

**To book Kelly for your next event, email her at <u>mykellyf@gmail.com</u> or visit her website at: <u>www.mykellyf.com</u> or blog: http://blog.mykellyf.com**

22578666R00089

Made in the USA
Charleston, SC
28 September 2013